From Dolmen Tombs to Heaven's Gate

Understanding World Heritage in Korea

Kim, Young Hoon

JIMOONDANG

Jimoondang
85 Gwanginsa-gil, Paju-si, Gyeonggi-do, 413-756, Korea
82 Donhwamun-ro, Jongno-gu, Seoul, 110-360, Korea
227 Suttons Lane, Edison, NJ 08817, USA
Phone: 82-2-743-3096 E-mail: edit@jimoon.co.kr
82-2-743-3192~3 E-mail: sale@jimoon.co.kr
Fax: 82-2-743-0227, 82-2-742-4657
Homepage: www.jimoon.co.kr

The National Library of Korea Cataloging-in-Publication (CIP)
From Dolmen Tombs to Heaven's Gate: Understanding World Heritage in Korea / by Kim, Young Hoon
Paju: Jimoondang, 2013
ISBN 978-89-6297-146-0 93900 911-KDC5 951.9-DDC21 CIP2013000557

Printed in Korea

Preface

A few years ago, our university asked me to design a course to introduce Korean culture in English. It was not only due to the increase in the number of exchange students from foreign countries but also to meet rising demand for domestic students to promote Korean culture to foreigners. I easily accepted the offer but it was not a simple task to satisfy both groups of students. Considering the fact that I spend only one semester with students, I had to ponder "what would be the best topics to share with them?" After brainstorming for a long time, I came up with the theme of 'World Cultural Heritage of Korea.' It was a strategy based on the idea of naturally dealing with overall Korean art, history and culture by exploring each Korean UNESCO World Heritage. However, there were still some remaining problems, "Would it be enough to cover all the materials only in the lecture room?"

After all, I designed a class integrating diverse factors such as several field trips, students' active participation, auditing videos and discussions as well as my lectures. I usually receive feedback from students after each semester. There were a few complaints in which students felt it was a burden to take field trips during the semester. Also, compared to other courses, more preparation was needed for the class. But a lot of foreign students who took my courses mentioned that they will never forget the pleasant memories of visiting historical sites. In fact, even for the majority of domestic students, it was their first visit to the historical sites so they were as impressed and learnt a great deal from the exploration. Moreover, there was an enthusiastic group of students who wanted to visit more historical sites. Somewhat extreme suggestions were also found in the students' feedbacks that the University should provide a shuttle bus for the course! I cannot help but smile thinking of the classes I had with the students and can still vividly remember their faces from time to time. Out of my intention, it has become a tradition to take a group photo in front of Jongmyo Jeongjeon and those photos make me think again of the meaning of this course.

What do I want from this course? I want to stress that even though we are to study world heritage in Korea, we should not just boast of them. Globally-valued architecture and historical records of Korea should be more universally studied and publicized. When we explore the cultural heritage of a particular region, we not only gain its knowledge but are further guided to broader questions as well. For example, we are likely to continue questioning "How are the characteristics of Korean Changdeokgung Palace similar or different from other palaces in near East Asian countries such as China and Japan?" or "What are the unique features of Korean Changdeokgung palace that makes it different from palaces in Western countries?" Thus, I consider that every question can help us to have a more profound and broader view toward the world and feel the special value in the history of humankind. I expect that such trials ultimately become the passage to every person in the world, not just limited to the studies of certain eras or regions.

This book is written for my class, "Understanding World Heritage in Korea." I would like to express my special gratitude to Jimoondang for willingly deciding to publish this book although it is not for pursuing profits. I also would like to thank my research assistant Nayoung Jeong and Jaerin Ahn for their help in collecting materials and Jeongeun Bae and Yoojin Shin for editing and revising. Last but not least, I give special thanks to my colleague, Professor Heather Willoughby, for her dedication in proofreading the manuscript and giving advice with Korean Romanization of the book, but more than anything, I feel gratitude toward her for providing a wonderful title for this book, *From Dolmen Tombs to Heaven's Gate: Understanding World Heritage in Korea.*

Contents

Royal

Confucian

Shrine in the

Joseon

Dynasty

(1392-1910)

Jongmyo Shrine

Let's begin our exploration into the world heritage of Korea. Our first stop in this journey is Jongmyo.

Where is Jongmyo in the first place? One of the charms of Seoul is that tradition and modernity are converged together in the structures. Jongmyo seems to be rather hidden in the bustling city center of Seoul. It is protected by high walls and a lush forest, and thus it is not easily seen from the outside. Compared to other favorite tourist spots in the city, its outward appearance is rather plain and even dull. But its historic importance is far beyond other sites. In my view, Jongmyo was the foundation of the Joseon Dynasty that epitomizes the spirit and ideology of Confucianism.

Yeongnyeongjeon
The Hall of Eternal Peace,
an auxiliary shrine

What is Jongmyo?

We must then ask... what is Jongmyo? What is Confucianism? Before we walk into the site, let me briefly explain the history and basic function of Jongmyo.

Jongmyo is simply the royal shrine of the Joseon Dynasty (1392-1910). It was built to enshrine royal ancestral spirit tablets and serve as the site for memorial services to the Joseon kings and queens.[1] What is surprising is that its basic function has been maintained through to the present. The Joseon Dynasty lasted 508 years, following its founding by King Taejo through the rule of the 27th monarch, King Sunjong. The royal ancestral rituals have been carried out at Jongmyo for more than 600 years, since the founding of the Joseon Dynasty until now. Its construction began in 1394. With the increasing number of enshrined spirit tablets, the number of buildings increased steadily throughout the Joseon era. According to historical records, the existing building was extended and new buildings were constructed at least eight times. Jongmyo was registered on the UNESCO World Heritage List in 1995.

1 Jongmyo Jeryeak, the memorial services conducted each year at the main shrine, Jeongjeon, is a comprehensive intangible cultural heritage which combines music, song, and dance.

Confucianism: The Core Purpose of Jongmyo

The Joseon Dynasty cannot be conceived without Confucianism, which was the founding ideology of the period. The most respected value in Confucianism is filial piety. According to this value, a new dynasty should construct a royal shrine to worship ancestors and pray for an affluent society. This royal shrine is to be built to the left of the royal palace. In addition, a king is to build a Sajik, a temple for the guardian deities of the State on the right of the palace.[2] Thus, it means that the founder of Joseon Dynasty, King Taejo, built Jongmyo even before his own palace.

In a Confucian society, performing rituals is the principle discipline of society and the basis of the reign. There are various types of rituals, among which sacrificial rites are the most important. The rites at Jongmyo were the most

2
Sa, god of Earth, and Jik, god of Harvest, were the two guardian deities of the Joseon Dynasty, and Sajikdan was the place where the king offered worship to these two guardian deities.

Jongmyo Jerye
It is the first of South Korea's Masterpieces of the Oral and Intangible Heritage of Humanity designated by UNESCO in 2001.

important ceremonies of the Joseon Dynasty. Jongmyo and Sajik represent the root of the Dynasty, and the worship at Jongmyo and Sajik implies the respect for ancestors and the legitimate reign of the king. Worship for ancestors leads to filial duties and further expands the notion of loyalty to the king and kingdom. By regularly organizing sacrificial rites, the people of the Joseon Dynasty were educated to assume their filial duties towards their parents and be loyal to their king. In this context, Jongmyo became the most important place in the Joseon Dynasty.

Architecture of Symbolism

As noted, Jongmyo is essentially a ritual place. For this reason, buildings should not be elaborately decorated; the architectural style of the buildings at Jongmyo can be reduced to simplicity. The structure of the buildings and their ornaments symbolize respect for ancestors. They do not contain any excessive space or additional structure. In particular, the large stone steps symbolize stability, the long lines of pillars symbolize the eternity of the throne, and the roof symbolizes infinity. Personally, Jongmyo is the best place for black and white photography.

Without any further delay, let's enter Jongmyo.

Jongmyo is composed of three sets of buildings centered around Jeongjeon (the main shrine), Yeongnyeongjeon (the Hall of Eternal Peace, an auxiliary shrine), Hyangdaecheong (a one story building for storing dishes and utensils used in the rituals), and others. In addition, there are three ponds and a well in order to get pure water for the rites.

As we enter through the main gate, there is a long outstretched pathway for us to follow.[3] This main road is composed of three lanes that have different heights.[4] The middle lane, which is the highest, is called Sinhyangno, literally meaning the divine pathway, which was reserved for the souls of the royal ancestors. Obviously, people should not walk on this lane. The left and right sides of Sinhyangno were the paths that the king and young princes passed through.

The distinctive feature of the lane is that the surface is rough and uneven. Why? Was it to cut down on the expenses and pay attention to the most important building, Jongmyo? It's absolutely not so. They had an underlying intention even in making the steps to have a solemn ritual. When you enter Jongmyo, you have to pay attention to the roads that they are not meaningless but actually designed according to the ritual

Jeongjeon
It is the main hall where the royal ancestral tablets are kept.

3
The main entrance to Jongmyo is called Changyeommun. It measures 3 kan in length and 2 kan in width. (A kan is a traditional unit of measurement, apporoxmately 1.8 meters, indicating the space between two pillars.)

4
The paths within Jongmyo are 4-8 meters in width and measure a total of 1,565 meters in length. Each pathway leads from the front gate to different buildings.

5
Jeongjeon is a wooden structure measuring 19 kan in length, 3 kan in width, and 3 kan along both the left and right wing chambers. It measures a total length of 1,270 meters with a frontal height of 10.14 meters. The east and west wings reach forward into the court platform like arms.

order and the movement of participants. To borrow the words of a famous architect, "Jongmyo can be defined in a word, architecture of the road."

Jeongjeon is the main hall where the royal ancestral tablets are kept.[5] Ancestors who passed away were considered almost like deities. For this reason, Jeongjeon is often compared to the Parthenon in Athens. Jeongjeon is surrounded by rectangular walls with gates to the south, east, and west. The rectangular inner court platform *woldae* is covered with rough slabs of granite. A pathway runs from the main gate, across the woldae, to the stone foundation of the main hall.

As time passed, an extension was needed to make room for

Sinhyangno
Literally meaning the divine pathway which was reserved for the souls of the royal ancestors.

The rear brick wall of
Jeongjeon

keeping more royal ancestral tablets. As a result, Jeongjeon was gradually expanded to a final 19 rooms. With the addition of the extensions, this building has been considered the longest building in the world, if we consider it as a single structure. At both ends of Jeongjeon, a room is annexed with servants' quarters located in the east and west. After several extensions since 1395, the total length of Jeongjeon is around 101 meters. It is hard to understand the impression that the length of Jongmyo gives when just looking at a photo of it. It looks simple but the harmony of the building, roof, woldae and the walls takes people's breath away due to its magnificence. Without any fancy decorations or high buildings, it still reveals a unique spirit and charm.

The long lines of pillars symbolize the eternity of the dynasty

Look at the lengthy roof. Jeongjeon is characterized by its

roof. Tiles laid on the roof makes 40 degrees angle and gives a unique impression. The front of the building is shaded and it adds allure and mystery. The magnificent sight that occurs when rain comes pouring down from the roof on a day of heavy rain is well known to professional photographers. When you look at the edge of the roof, you will find small statues called "Japsang." Japsang are clay figures derived from

The lengthy roof of Jeongjeon

a popular Chinese story that were built on the ridge of the roof in order to expel evil spirits.

Let's look inside. After all, everything including the wide woldae, long roof and lined up pillars is only for ancestral tablets that are preserved deep inside the building. At the innermost part of the building, there is Sinsil, the inner shrine room, where the royal ancestral tablets of both kings and queens are kept. To see the royal ancestral tablets, you have to

Toekan (open corridor)

enter Sinsil and go through a few layers of protective covers; the tablets are preserved in the wooden boxes.

The royal ancestral tablets were taken out during ancestral rituals and shown only to the royal family and religious service managers in the Joseon Dynasty. The wooden tablets were so precious that they were the first thing in which kings must take care of, even if a war broke out. It was believed that the royal ancestral tablets enshrined the spirits of the ancestors.

Auxiliary building, Yeongnyeongjeon, was built in 1431 which is smaller than Jeongjeon but it has a similar design and structure. The tablets of deceased monarchs were removed from Jeongjeon after a set period of time and placed in Yeongnyeongjeon. In addition, Yeongnyeongjeon enshrines the tablets of four generations of King Taejo's ancestors,

Sinsil
Inner shrine room

Royal spirit tablet

posthumously honored with the title of king, and kings who had fallen into disfavor. A total of 34 tablets are enshrined in the 16 rooms.

Apart from Jeongjeon and Yeongnyeongjeon, additional buildings exist, including Chilsadang and Gongsindang where the tablets of meritorious retainers are kept, Jaesil where the king prepared for the rites, Jeonsacheong where ritual vessels and other impliments are kept, and Akgongcheong where musicians waited for the rites.

Why is Jongmyo Considered a World Heritage?

Jongmyo is an ancestral shrine housing the memorial tablets of the kings and queens of the Joseon Dynasty. It is a precious cultural heritage by which Confucianism, the ruling ideology of the Joseon Dynasty, patriotism and filial piety, have been passed down to the present. Then, what is the universal value of Jongmyo in the context of world culture?

Jongmyo's architectural characteristics and the continued preservation of the rituals in their original form have served as the basic framework for Korea's spiritual tradition as well as for East Asian ethics in general, and therefore, serve as a valuable cultural heritage that should be permanently preserved. As discussed, Jongmyo's architectural style is very unique for its length, which emphasizes horizontal lines and hence differs radically from that of China, the birthplace of Confucian royal ancestral shrine architecture. Indeed, such architecture is rarely found anywhere in the world.

In addition, the ritual, Jongmyo Jerye, was first standardized in 1462 and has been passed down nearly intact for over 550 years, making it the world's oldest comprehensive cultural ritual. It is a vivid example that an intangible cultural heritage can breathe the vitality into historical architecture.

Reference

Deuchler, Martina.1992. *The Confucian Transformation of Korea: A Study of Society and Ideology.* Cambridge, MA: Harvard University Press.

Shin, Myung-ho, Timothy V. Atkinson (trans.). 2004. *Joseon Royal Court Culture: Ceremonial and Daily Life.* Paju: Dolbegae Publishers.

Jongmyo Shrine - UNESCO World Heritage Centre, http://whc.unesco.org/en/list/738

Palace

of

Illustrious

Virtue

Changdeokgung Palace

Palace! When you hear the word, what is the first thing that comes to your mind? Grandeur? Royal families? Mysteries? Palaces have attracted many people in the world for different reasons.

What is your favorite palace in the world? Buckingham Palace in London, the Forbidden City in Beijing or Schönbrunn Palace in Austria may be among your choices.

People have always been fascinated by majestic palaces, for their beauty and their long history. Every palace contains many important architectural and cultural characteristics, which reflect each dynasty in history.

Now, let me introduce to you my favorite, namely, Changdeokgung Palace in Seoul, Korea.

What are the Architectural Distinctive Features of Changdeokgung Palace?

Changdeokgung Palace is the only one among five palaces found in Seoul that was designated as a UNESCO World Heritage in 1996. Why not the others? In order to answer this question, we need to look at the architectural and historical importance of Changdeokgung Palace.

The construction of Changdeokgung Palace, the "Palace of Illustrious Virtue," began in 1405 as a detached palace of Gyeongbokgung Palace, which was built as the main palace of the newly founded Joseon Dynasty in 1394. Several royal palaces were originally built by the kings of the Joseon Dynasty to prepare for wars and disasters; there were a few

Geumcheongyo
The oldest stone bridge in Seoul

more palaces, apart from today's remaining "Five Grand Palaces." During the Japanese invasion of Korea in 1592, Changdeokgung Palace was ruined, but it was rebuilt from 1607 to 1610. Since that time, Changdeokgung Palace served as the government headquarter and the royal residence. Gyeongbokgung Palace was left in disrepair until it was restored in 1868, when King Gojong moved the court back there in the 5th year of his reign. Changdeokgung Palace served as the seat of power of the Joseon Dynasty for a total of 258 years. It has been the main stage of the history of Joseon for the longest time and it is a precious heritage that best embodies the royal culture of the Joseon Dynasty.

Changdeokgung Palace preserves the original architectural form and design of East Asian palaces. Its excellence exists in the architectural beauty that is in harmony with nature.

A mythical creature at one of the pillars of Geumcheongyo

Changdeokgung Palace in Korea and the Forbidden City in China are both registered on the UNESCO World Heritage List. Although these two palaces are constructed according to the East Asian cultural design, they have more differences than similarities. While the Forbidden City is at the pinnacle of artificial beauty, Changdeokgung Palace is a masterpiece of naturalism. The Forbidden City overwhelms people and becomes the symbol of the authority of the Emperor. On the contrary, Changdeokgung Palace illustrates dignity but does not give an overwhelming impression; rather it provides a comfortable feeling with its harmony with nature.

Thus, it can be said that Changdeokgung Palace is a monument built by men but which displays the aspiration of nature as well. The whole palace compound is broadly divided into two areas, one containing the palace buildings and the other constituting the rear garden. High palace walls enclose the entire compound.

There is one thing that we should all know before we enter Changdeokgung Palace. It is the painting *Donggwoldo*. It is a historical artifact which presents the features of Changdeokgung Palace of the 1830s in detail. It is unknown exactly when and who drew it but it testifies to the size and incomparable beauty of the palace. It is unquestionably a masterwork that illustrates the palace which was also called "Donggwol" because it was situated in the east. The painting is 584 centimeters wide and 273 centimeters long.

Now, let's go inside the palace and see more in detail.

The grand Donhwamun Gate stands due south at the front entrance, opening to a wide path. This gate is the oldest wooden structure in Changdeokgung Palace; after the

Japanese invasion, it was rebuilt in 1607 and has remained since then. A few steps through the gate brings one to Geumcheongyo, the Silky Stream Bridge, which is an east-west oriented structure. The bridge, which has remained since it was first built, is the oldest stone bridge not only in Changdeokgung Palace but also in the entire city of Seoul.

In order to enter Changdeokgung Palace, one has to pass this bridge. If a bridge in a Buddhist temple is a liaison between the world of ordinary people and the world of Buddha, Geumcheongyo, the bridge at Changdeokgung Palace, is a demarcation line between an ordinary outside and a sacred inside. Four stone sculptures of unknown animals are placed at each of the four pillars of the bridge respectively. They even make us feel the warmth with their naive smiles and cute gestures. A stone sculpture of an animal and the face of a bogy are also originals.

Walking along the path to the right, you will encounter the Injeongmun Gate. From that gateway, the grandeur of Injeongjeon, the throne hall, strikes one's eye. Injeongjeon is one of the most imposing buildings in the palace. Set on a double terrace, this two story throne hall is upheld by huge columns with a corbelled multibracket eave system. It has a single high ceilinged hall inside and staircases leading to the interior balcony which circles around the four sides of the upper story level.

As a result of the influx of Western civilization in the 19th century, rather modern chandeliers now illuminate the hall. Backed by a screen on which are drawn the sun and the moon, symbolizing royalty, and five peaks, symbolizing the whole nation, the elaborate throne is placed on a raised dais

Donggwoldo

A bird's-eye view of Changdeokgung Palace (the Eastern Palace)

(Source: Korea University Museum)

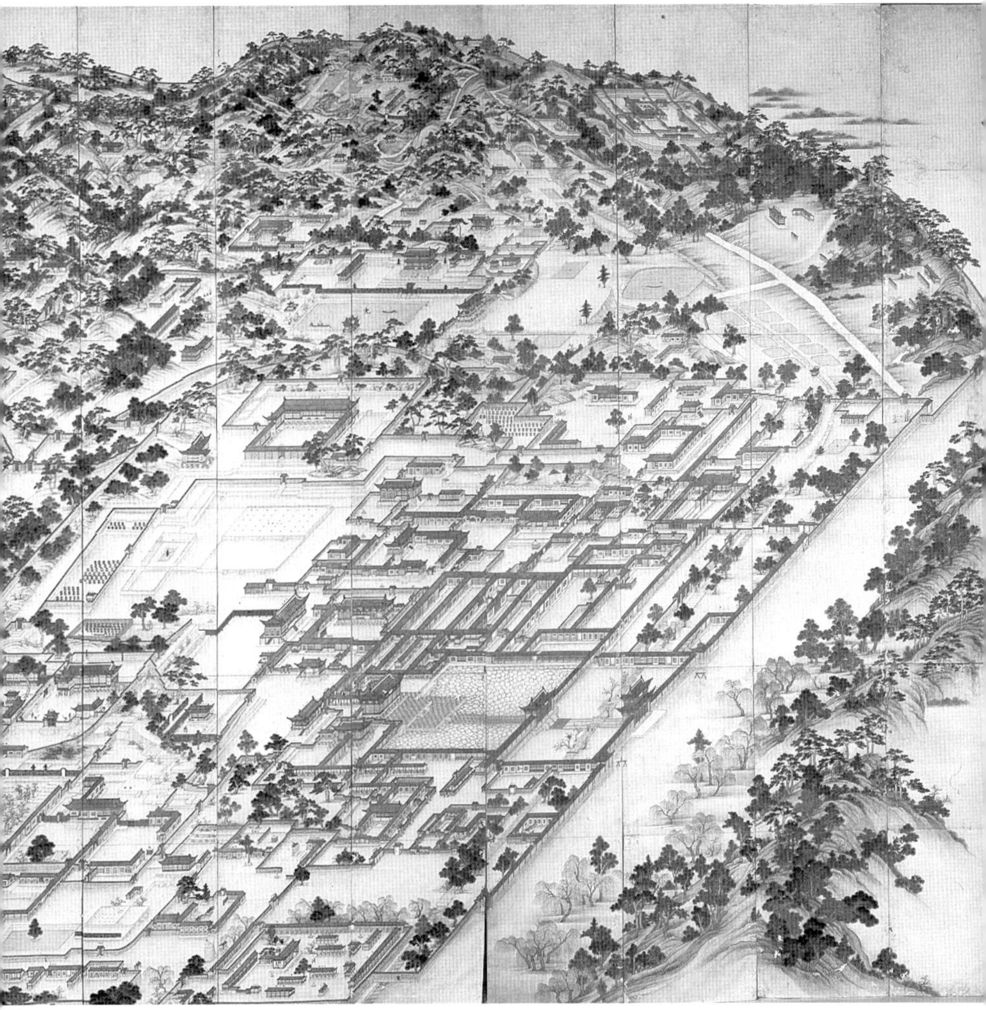

below an intricately fretworked wooden platform with an ornamental dragon design. A series of small posts stand in the court marking the ranks of the hierarchy of governmental service, from the senior and junior grades of the first rank to those of ninth rank civilian officials on the east and military officers on the west.

Passing through the long corridors to the east is the elegant Seonjeongjeon. This is the king's office where the king discussed the affairs of the dynasty. This building is characterized by the blue tiles on the roof. This is the historical significance behind why the current Presidential office is still called "Cheong-wadae" meaning "an office with a blue tiled roof." Next door to the east is Huijeongdang, the hall containing the king's residence. The current Huijeongdang looks much different than its original state. After a fire in 1917, the building was moved from Gyeongbokgung Palace and rebuilt; it looks different from the past, and electricity and western furniture are in place. A western style porch is added in front of the building to make it easier to get on or off cars. For this, quite a lot of palace buildings were removed and now replaced by a lawn. Behind the king's residence is Daejojeon, the queen's residence.

The queen's residence was placed in the innermost part of the palace and it was prohibited to enter the building and it was even taboo to look at the area. Maybe queens were the ones who had the least amount of freedom despite their high position. In the back of the building, there is the largest garden in Changdeokgung Palace and it is indeed the most beautiful place. It is the place where you can enjoy four distinct seasons with the beautiful scenery of trees, flowers and the fantastic shapes of stones. Above all, a terraced flower bed is uniquely designed so as to keep the original form of the hilly terrain. If you climb the stairs and stand at the top, you can see the roof of palaces and the landscapes outside of the palace. It shows a thoughtful consideration for the queen.

The Secret Garden is the zenith of Korean landscape gardening, a sylvan sanctuary with rare trees transplanted from across the country as well as indigenous trees, pavilions and reflecting ponds. The Secret Gardern is composed of areas such as Buyongji Pond, Aeryeonji Pond and Ongnyucheon Stream.

Aeryeonjeong Pavilion in winter
(Source: Changdeokgung Palace)

Buyongji, the Lotus Pond

Within the Secret Garden, the Buyongji area is the most beautiful landscape. In this rectangular pond floats an artificial mountain which symbolizes a mountain deity. King Jeongjo built this pond in 1792, together with Buyongjeong Pavillion, Juhamnu Court Library and Yonghwadang Pavillion around the pond.

If you look at one of the surrounding stone pillars, you can find the image of a fish carved into it. The carved image of a fish jumping out of the water is very lively. Then why did they carve the fish image? The answer lies in the name of the gate which stands on the way to Juhamnu. The gate is known as "Eosumun" literally meaning "the gate of fish and water." The name reflects the wisdom that a fish cannot live out of water. It was meant to remind kings that a ruler must always consider his people.

Buyongjeong Pavilion
The pavilion has a peculiar roof, doors and ceilings, and every corner has elegant touches.
(Source: The Academy of Korean Studies)

Eosumun

Buyongjeong Pavilion

The beautiful and unique Buyongjeong Pavilion is a multisided wooden structure, basically designed to represent the shape of a Chinese character (亞), which is often used in latticed paper doors. The fully-blossomed-lotus-flower-like structure with a raised floor dips its two legs into the lotus pond. Decorative wooden balustrades rail its balcony. Its peculiar roof, doors, ceilings and all corners are well finished with elegant touches that tell us that this pavilion is an architectural treasure of Korea.

Bulnomun Gate
The stone gate, Bulnomun, was established for wishing eternal life for the kings.

Aeryeonji Pond and Aeryeonjeong Pavilion

Before you get to Aeryeonji Pond, there is a stone gate that you pass through. This gate is called "Bulnomun" and testifies of the desire for eternal life for the kings. It is famous because it was carved from a single boulder.

At the northern rim of Aeryeonji Pond is Aeryeonjeong Pavilion which was built in 1692. The pyramidal roof is capped with a cupola and its four false hip rafters are edged with dragonhead tiles. The dragon heads were used to prevent fires, since the dragon was believed to preside over water and therefore prevent fire. Over the ridge of the pond is a more naturallooking pond called "Bandoji," and many delightful pavilions are hidden away in the nearby woods.

Aeryeonji Pond
Aeryeonjeong Pavilion
The name of a pond and a pavilion, Aeryeon, means "loving the lotus," which symbolizes the virtue of a gentleman.

Ongnyucheon Stream

This stream flows all the way through the innermost heart of the garden. It circles around a water course on Soyoam Rock under the well and gurgles down. On the face of a small boulder on Soyoam is inscribed "Ongnyucheon" in the handwriting of King Injo. Above is a quatrain which says, "The stream ascends three hundreds leagues to heaven, falls down again, spans a white rainbow, and casts lightening and resonant thunder all over the valley." Cheonguijeong, Soyojeong, Chwihanjeong and other pavilions are scattered around this spot.

Soyoam Rock and Ongnyucheon Stream
Ongnyucheon means the stream of clear jade water. This area was a secret garden with rocks and a stream only for the kings.

Cheonguijeong Pavilion
Among the five pavilions in the Ongnyucheon area, it is the only pavilion that has a thatched roof with a small rice field laid out before it.

Why is Changdeokgung Palace Considered a World Heritage?

The whole Changdeokgung Palace compound is the epitome of a rich Korean legacy. It preserves numerous examples of superb architecture, national treasures and ancient trees as natural monuments. Changdeokgung Palace reflects sophisticated values harmonized with beautiful surroundings. To present the authority of the king over the nation, palace buildings, especially Changdeokgung Palace, were built with the utmost architectural skill, creative design and garden landscaping.

Changdeokgung Palace is different from other palaces of the Joseon Dynasty that were built to follow a symmetrical layout to accentuate the authority of the king. It was freed from this principle. Donhwamun, the main gate, faces due south. Crossing Geumcheongyo Bridge to the east takes one to a path leading north to the throne hall, which faces south. The administrative court and the king's private quarters are all spread out to the east until the throne hall; all of the buildings are mapped without consideration for the usual fixed principles of geomancy. Because one of the ridges called "Eungbong," the Palace's main guardian mountain, stretches down to the east side of the compound, the palace was naturally able to make the best use of these topological conditions without major excavation. As a result, the palace buildings, pavilions and ponds are snuggled exquisitely throughout the sylvan woodland, the hills and streams.

Out of all the palaces during the Joseon period, Changdeokgung Palace was the seat of the dynasty for the longest time. With its beautiful architecture harmonized with the picturesque landscape, it achieved the acme of perfection. In this regard, the palace deserves to be preserved as a world heritage.

Reference

Han, Young Woo, Jae-suk Kim (trans.). 2007. *Donggwoldo: Painting of Eastern Palace: Changdoekgung and Changgyeonggung.* Paju: Hyohyung Publishers.

Ministry of Culture & Sports. 1996. *Changdeokgung Palace*. World Heritage List Application. Government of Republic of Korea.

Park, Hyung-yu. 2010. *An Ethnographic study of Changdeok palace: heritage tourism and symbolic representations of national identity.* Paju, Korea: Jimoondang.

Yu, Gary. 2000. Changdokkung: the Palace of Illustrious Virtue in Seoul. *World heritage review*, 15, pp. 18-29.

Changdeokgung Palace Complex, http://eng.cdg.go.kr

Changdeokgung Palace - UNESCO World Heritage Centre, http://whc.unesco.org/en/list/816

Korea University Museum

The Academy of Korean Studies

Brilliant
Fortress
of
Suwon

Suwon Hwaseong Fortress

Suwon Hwaseong Fortress was designated as a World Heritage by UNESCO in 1997. So what is Suwon Hwaseong Fortress? Where is it? Why was the fortress selected as a world heritage despite the fact that most of it was remade? (It is a replica! Not an original.)

In this section, these questions will be answered and hopefully by the end of the chapter you will have a better understanding about this beautiful and magnificent world heritage of Korea.

Where is Suwon Hwaseong Fortress Located?

1
The city of Suwon is located 30 kilometers south of Seoul and the fortress surrounds most of the central area of Suwon today.

The very first thing to know about this historical site is its location. Suwon Hwaseong Fortress is located in Suwon[1], Gyeonggi Province of South Korea.

The fortress sprawls over both flat and hilly terrain. The eastern part of the fortress is on flat ground, while the western part lies on Paldalsan Mountain. Such a position gave the fortress a military advantage. A building, when placed on a plain, is very vulnerable to external attacks. That is why during wartime, kings went to their fortresses in the mountain, rather than staying in their palaces located in the plains. By placing the fortress on the western part of Paldalsan mountain, Suwon Hwaseong Fortress was able to serve as both a palace and a fortress.

Why was Suwon Hwaseong Fortress Constructed?

Poru
A sentry tower

There were several reasons for the construction of the Suwon Hwaseong Fortress. First of all, King Jeongjo, the 22nd King of the Joseon Dynasty, built Suwon Hwaseong Fortress out of

Janganmun

The northern gate of Suwon Hwaseong Fortress

長安

filial piety. Prince Sado, the father of Jeongjo, died after being locked alive in a rice chest by his own father, King Yeongjo. In order to honor his father and move his grave to a more auspicious site, King Jeongjo decided to relocate the tomb to Suwon and build a fortress nearby.

But more importantly, Prince Sado's tragic death weakened

Banghwasuryujeong Pavilion

the power of King Jeongjo when he was first crowned the king. In order to regain the authority of the king and eradicate party conflicts, he wanted to move the capital from Seoul to Suwon. Suwon was in a strategic position that connected Seoul with the Yellow Sea and China. King Jeongjo felt Suwon had the potential to become a prosperous new capital.

King Jeongjo even changed the name from Suwonbu to Hwaseong, literally meaning a "Brilliant Fortress." Chae Je-

Gong, a former minister, and Jo SimTae, the superintendent, fully carried out the project between January 1794 and September 1796 with the help of scholars of the Practical Learning (Silhak) school, such as Jeong YakYong, who was well acquainted with mechanical devices that helped to facilitate the construction. The practical planner Jeong YakYong referred to the theories of both Western and Eastern fortress designs and made fruitful achievements by integrating the knowledge and technology of his time. He meticulously took the effectiveness of construction process as well as the physical design of fortress into consideration.

What are the Basic Structures of Suwon Hwaseong Fortress?

Within Suwon Hwaseong Fortress, it is possible to see a variety of military as well as artistic structures. The main structures of the fortress include four gates and an expansive stone wall in addition to other structures that will be mentioned briefly.

Suwon Hwaseong Fortress has four gates corresponding to the four cardinal directions, Janganmun (north) and Paldalmun (south) are the larger of the four main gates and are topped with two story wooden pavilions while Hwaseomun (west) and Changnyongmun (east) are smaller and, therefore, have

華虹門

only one-story pavilions. Each gate is surrounded by the notable Ongseong. These ongseongs are semicircle fortifications that protect each gate.

Frequently along the wall, it is possible to see small openings facing straight out, from which it was possible to either shoot arrows out or other smaller holes that emptied out below, in case the fortress was under attack. Guards were able to patrol all around the fortress by walking along this wall and could quickly alert others if enemies approached; however, there is no record of it having been used since there was no actual battle fought at Suwon Hwaseong Fortress.

Along the wall and within the fortress other structures are present. These include: a floodgate, four secret gates, four guard platforms, two observation towers, two command posts, two archers' platforms, five firearm bastions, five sentry posts and a beacon tower.

Seobuk Gongsimdon, the northwest observation tower
This four-sided tower is empty inside. Many gun embrasures on all sides allow watching for enemy movement and for firing cannons, rifles and bows.

What Made the Construction of Suwon Hwaseong Fortress Unique?

When analyzing any artificial structure, it is always interesting to see what characteristics make the particular structure unique. In doing so, it is necessary to consider the materials used, the process in which the materials were applied, and finally the tools used in order to bring the drawing plans to life as the actual physical structure. The case of Suwon Hwaseong Fortress is no different. When examining the Fortress, the construction materials as well as the construction process made the building quite unique in comparison to other similar structures around the world. The fairly new building materials and techniques employed to create the fortress had not been widely used in Korea prior to the Suwon Hwaseong Fortress construction.

Suwon Hwaseong Fortress was constructed using a mix of materials in order for the fortress to fulfill its purpose of withstanding the most extravagant attacks that the enemies had to offer. The mix of stone, timber and bricks provided a solid foundation and made the walls sturdy and strong against attacks up close and from afar. Bricks had not been used extensively in Korea prior to the construction of the fortress. Thus, the use of bricks was very innovative during the time it was built. The reason the bricks were used rather than just stones was fairly simple yet ingenious. If the fortress was hit by cannonball, only a small portion would crumble and be destroyed rather than the whole wall collapsing, and subsequently exposing the inside to the enemy.

Hence, this foreign import proved to be a superior way of building the fortified walls that King Jeongjo wanted. In addition to the brick walls, the tools employed by the construction workers make Suwon Hwaseong Fortress unique. During the construction process, various advanced pieces of equipment such as the *Geojunggi* were used to transport the large rocks and heavy loads of bricks as well as timber to the construction site. This alleviated stress on the life of the workers by reducing the amount of physical labor required as well as permitted the use of large stones to strengthen the fortress walls.

Due to the construction materials and building process, Suwon Hwaseong Fortress separated itself from other fortresses in the world. It is one of the most scientific, well-designed fortresses in Asia. However, what we see today of these amazing structures are not the originals built in the 18th century. Instead they are a replica from the reconstruction conducted in the 1970s. After a lot of damage was accrued during the Japanese colonization and Korean War, much of the fortress had to be rebuilt. However, each of these reconstructed buildings has been meticulously and identically rebuilt to restore it to its previous state.

Authenticity and the state of preservation are very important factors needed to be recognized as World Heritage; the fact that Suwon Hwaseong Fortress was heavily destroyed and the original appearance of the buildings and walls were lost was regarded as a critical flaw. When the UNSECO inspectors came to examine the fortress and consider its registration as a World Heritage, their primary concern was whether it had been faithfully restored to its original state. After being shown the original construction blueprint and seeing how intricate the records inside it were, as well as how the workers had followed the plans precisely in the process of restoring the fortress, the structure was deemed authentic. What is this construction blueprint, the so called "Hwaseong seongyeok uigwe?"

What is Hwaseong seongyeok uigwe?

Hwaseong seongyeok uigwe (the Uigwe henceforth) is the archives for the construction of Suwon Hwaseong Fortress. It is a detailed account of the whole construction process, including all the architectural and engineering procedures employed in the construction of the fortress, including pictures of the structural design, dimensions of the structure, the uses and sources of the materials, and other minor details of the project. Even the materials and costs required to build the equipment were recorded. The book also recorded a list of all the artisans from the stonemasons to the carpenters who participated in the construction; even the number of days they worked and what they worked on was recorded.

Another notable feature of the records is the rich illustrations. Together with paintings that depict the various stages

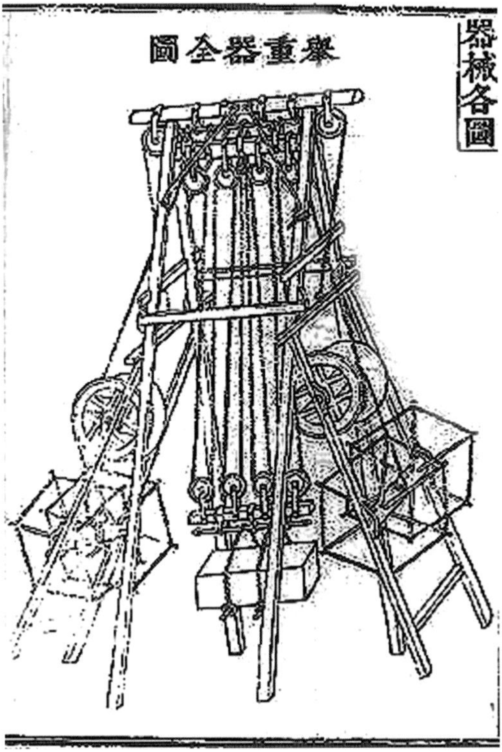

Illustration of Geojunggi in the records of Hwaseong seongyeok uigwe

of different ceremonies, diagrams of the buildings and articles used are, without exception, included in the Uigwe. Even after hundreds of years, the pictures in the Uigwe have not been discolored and still exhibit the vivid yet calm shades unique to natural colorings.

The Uigwe was published in 1801 after the completion of Suwon Hwaseong Fortress. It is highly appraised due to its historical value; the book is an achievement without parallel in the history of world architecture.

Why is Hwaseong Fortress Considered a World Heritage?

Suwon Hwaseong Fortress was enlisted on the World Heritage List during the 21st general assembly of the World Heritage Committee held in Italy in 1997. During this meeting, the Executive Committee concluded that the Suwon Hwaseong Fortress was a remarkable military facility of the early modern age, which showed sophisticated architectural technologies and scientific knowhow. The International Council of Heritage also stressed the importance of this fortress, saying "Suwon Hwaseong Fortress is a representative military construction of the 18th century and shows the combination of Western and East Asian technology."

It will be interesting to compare the fortress with ones on the opposite site of the world. One of the examples of the Western military architecture built in the 18th century is Suomenlinna, the Fortress of Finland. This exclusive bastion fortress was inscribed as the UNESCO World Heritage in 1991. Suomenlinna represents the general theory of fortifications in European countries as well as its special features that required unique technology to build it on a highly variable terrain.

Suwon Hwaseong Fortress has meaning beyond a military installation. The fortress is an artistic figure as well as a military facility; at the same time, it is a comprehensive project that embraces the entire city of Suwon. As mentioned earlier, the preliminary design and the building process of Suwon Hwaseong Fortress was one of the best construction projects that presented the convergence of both contemporary knowledge and scientific technology.

Reference

Asian Historical Architecture, http://www.orientalarchitecture.com

Suwon Hwaseong Fortress - UNESCO World Heritage Centre, http://whc.unesco.org/en/list/817

Hwaseong Haenggung, http://ehs.suwon.ne.kr

Suwon City Hall

Woodblocks

of the Goryeo Dynasty

and

Storage Halls

Tripitaka Koreana and Janggyeong Panjeon in Haeinsa Temple

Haeinsa Temple is one of the primary temples of Korean Buddhism. It is situated in Gayasan Mountain, one of Korea's most beautiful mountains which because of its rugged terrain has remained immune to the ravages of war. The literal meaning of Haeinsa is "Temple of Reflection on a Smooth Sea," which is an important image in Buddhist thought. When the mind is free from the wild waves of worldly desires and follies, it will attain calmness in which the true image of all existence is clearly reflected.

Buddhism was first transmitted to East Asia through China, hence the first types of Buddhist scriptures to reach Korea were written in classical Chinese. There were several attempts by many countries to inscribe the texts onto wooden printing blocks for distribution; however, the Tripitaka[1] Koreana is the only complete canon still in existence in Asia. It is also one of the most comprehensive and oldest intact copies of Buddhist scriptures in the world. More than anything else, Haeinsa Temple[2] is famous for being the home of Tripitaka Koreana, storing more than 81,000 wooden blocks.

1
This Sanskrit name comes from the fact that ancient Buddhist texts were written on palm leaves and stored in baskets. The three parts of a Tripitaka include a Sutra Pitaka (Buddhist Scriptures), a Vinaya Pitaka (Precepts), and an Abhidharma (Discourse).

2
There are three main principle Buddhist temples in Korea, each representing one of the "Three Jewels of Buddhism." Tongdosa Temple represents the Buddha, because it has a famous pagoda that contains relics of the Buddha from China. Songgwangsa Temple represents Sangha or the Buddhist community. Finally, Haeinsa Temple represents the Dharma or the Buddha's teaching because it houses a large number of Buddhist scriptures.

What is the Tripitaka Koreana?

Tripitaka Koreana is called Palman daejanggyeong in Korean, which means eighty thousand Tripitaka. Tripitaka, a Sanskrit word meaning three baskets, in this case indicates a Korean collection of Buddhist scripture that were carved onto 82,258 wooden printing blocks in the 13th century. It is the world's most comprehensive and the oldest intact version of Buddhist canon without any errors in the 52,382,960 characters which are organized in over 1,496 titles and 6,558 volumes. Tripitaka Koreana is listed as a Memory of the World and the depository of Tripitaka Koreana has been designated as a UNESCO World Heritage site, in recognition of it being the most complete among all Buddhist doctrinal texts in the world and for the high aesthetic quality of its workmanship.

The historical value of Tripitaka Koreana comes from the fact that it is the most complete and accurate extant collection of Buddhist treatises, laws and scriptures. Every block was inscribed with 23 lines of text with 14 characters per line. Therefore, each block, counting both sides, contained a total of 644 characters.

Tripitaka Koreana is considered to be the most accurate of all extant Tripitaka texts using Chinese characters because Sugidaesa, the Buddhist monk in charge of the carving, thoroughly compared them with the contents of other extant texts, corrected errors and replaced missing characters.

What are the Unique Features of the Woodblocks of the Tripitaka Koreana?

The first Tripitaka Koreana was destroyed by the Mongolians in 1232, but because these woodblocks were so important to the king and his people that they decided to recreate them. The process to recreate the Tripitaka Koreana was very complex and it took a lot of time and planning.

The trees needed to be submerged in seawater for about

寺印

伽倻

one to two years and then were cut according to a specific plan and then were boiled in salt water. Through this process the resin of the tree was completely depleted and salt, which absorbs the water, was covered on the surface to preserve the wood as well as prevent and reduce cracks and distortion. This process also helped protect the boards from insects, splitting and bending. After being submerged and boiled in sea water, they were then dried in the shade and exposed

Janggyeong Panjeon
One of the oldest buildings on the temple grounds and is uniquely structured and designed for the natural preservation of the Tripitaka Koreana.

The front of Janggyeong Panjeon
An essential aspect of the building is the placement and size of the bar lattice windows.

to wind for another three years before making the surface smooth.

The prepared blocks were transported to a designated place for carving. The planning had to be perfect and so a lot of time and research were put into this project in order to make an accurate copy of the original Tripitaka Koreana. Monks and others made a manuscript for the sides of each block which consisted of 23 lines and 14 characters each and were unified in the form of a specific calligraphic style. This manuscript would then be attached to the block and carved accordingly.

Experienced engravers from all over the country were involved with this task and they bowed every time they carved a character. There are more than 5 million characters!

One of the mysteries of Tripitaka Koreana is that the entire collection of the woodblocks content is flawless. The reason

The bar lattice windows
These windows help provide a natural air circulation, allowing for an even flow of the outside air in and out of the building.

for this is because they checked each block before the final process of sealing.

For the final part of the process they attached thick wood clubs on both ends of block and decorated each corner with copper plates and framed them with metal to prevent the blocks from warping and to help maintain good air cir-

The Tripitaka Koreana woodblock
(Source: Haeinsa Temple)

culation. The completed blocks were then varnished with a lacquer, which was essential for keeping insects away and preventing corrosion for long term storage. The woodblocks of the Tripitaka Koreana have defied time and the elements, surviving the ravages of war and internal turmoil over the last seven centuries.

What is the Secret of Preservation?

The depository, Janggyeong Panjeon, is one of the oldest buildings on the temple grounds and is uniquely structured and designed for the natural preservation of the Tripitaka Koreana. Janggyeong Panjeon is notable in itself because it was constructed specifically for the storage of artifacts and it exhibits remarkably effective solutions developed in the 15th century for the problems posed by the need to preserve the woodblocks against deterioration.

The extraordinary features of the depository were designed to provide natural ventilation, to adjust to varying temperatures and humidity and to adapt to fluctuating climatic conditions, allowing for the preservation of the woodblocks. Every aspect of the architectural design was considered for the preservation, such as the placement of the windows, the natural materials used for building, even the placement and positioning of the building itself. This entire depository was devoted to preserving the Tripitaka Koreana woodblocks, so much so that these woodblocks seem as if they were made just yesterday.

Built at the highest point of the temple, 655 meters above sea level, Janggyeong Panjeon faces southwest to receive the greatest possible number of hours of sunlight, to avoid damp winds from the valley below, and it is shielded by mountain peaks from the cold north wind.

Different sized windows on the north and south sides of both main halls are used for ventilation, utilizing principles of aerodynamics. The upper lattice windows are smaller than the lower ones in the front. These are reversed in the back with the upper lattice windows larger than the lower ones. This placement provides a very natural air flow and circulation from the outside into the depository. The air current from the south comes through the small, lower lattice windows, circulates inside the stacks, then flows out the upper lattice window in the back of the building.

Janggyeong Panjeon's walls are finished with dirt and the floors are covered in layers of natural resources in order to control moisture levels. The ground is filled with natural substances such as lime mortar, charcoal, salt, clay, sand, plaster powder and yellow earth. These natural materials have contributed to maintaining an optimal level of humidity by establishing a system in which there is absorption during the summer and moisture emission in the winter.

Another important aspect that helps in controlling dampness and temperature are the shelves which are placed like books on a bookshelf in two layers, one on top of the other.

The block shelf has five shelves and blocks are arranged closely, thus, narrow spaces between the blocks produce a stack effect which in turn greatly affects the control of dampness and temperature.

Janggyeong Panjeon is a remarkable structure in that Korean ancestors developed such advanced technology by utilizing and harmonizing with nature. The technology from the Janggyeong Panjeon and from the Tripitaka Koreana carries the wisdom and displays the honor of the people who took part in the creation of this most prized cultural treasure.

Why are Tripitaka Koreana and Janggyeong Panjeon Considered World Heritages?

Tripitaka Koreana is surprising in two senses. First, it has an important historical meaning in the world history of printing and the cultural development of human beings. Second, it is conserved well enough to let us read its contents even 800 years later.[3]

As mentioned before, the comprehensiveness, artistry and historical significance of its contents are recognized as a world heritage. In a word, the Tripitaka Koreana is a universal intellectual storage.

3 Digital Tripitaka Koreana: Tripitaka Koreana, which was manually carved on woodblocks 800 years ago, can now be found on the Internet (www.sutra.re.kr). A CD-ROM version can be purchased as well. Haeinsa and Temple the Institute of Study on Tripitaka Koreana digitalized the original Tripitaka Koreana during a nine year period. The entire Tripitaka Koreana is now contained on nine CD-ROMs. The Tripitaka Koreana was previously published in 48 volumes and is possessed by major libraries throughout the world: The digitalization of the Tripitaka Koreana in 2000 makes it possible for everyone to keep one of the world cultural heritages in his / her own possession.

Janggyeong Panjeon was registered as a UNESCO World Cultural Heritage in 1995. Janggyeong Panjeon looks simple and shabby at first glance. Then what are the reasons for this storage facility to be designated as a world heritage? The remarkable scientific secrets are hidden all over the depositories for the Tripitaka Koreana. It is amazing how Korean ancestors utilized the principles of aerodynamics by using different sized windows for ventilation, regulating temperature and humidity of the building.

Janggyeong Panjeon, which is located at the highest point of Haeinsa Temple, has been highly valued because no other historical structure in the world is specifically dedicated to the preservation of Tripitaka.

One of the most used and renowned version of Tripitakas in the world is Taisho Tripitaka of Japan. Taisho Tripitaka was made in the early 20th century (1924-1934) by collecting and editing extant Tripitakas. It is the most updated version of Tripitaka; thus the most number of Buddhist canons are collected in this edition. It contains 100 volumes: Volumes 1-85 are the literature, volumes 86-97 includes Buddhist iconography, volumes 98-100 are indexes.

Reference

2011 Millennial Anniversary of the Tripitaka Koreana, http://eng.tripitaka2011.com

Haeinsa Temple

The Research Institute of Tripitaka Koreana, http://www.sutra.re.kr

Tripitaka Koreana, http://www.80000.or.kr

Megalithic
Monuments
of the Bronze Age

Gochang, Hwasun, Ganghwa Dolmen Sites

When people first see megalithic culture, such as dolmens, they would mostly ask two related questions: When and why these huge structures were built? There are more things about the megalithic culture of Korea that we don't know than we do. And one of the most surprising facts is that Korea has the greatest number of dolmens in the world.

Let's find out the answer to this interesting mystery of the ancient past of Korea.

Dolmen in Hwasun area

What is a Dolmen?

Just one of the countless forms of graves, a dolmen consists of a large covering stone that acts as a lid, with several stones propped up underneath to form a grave. Goindol, the Korean word for dolmen, is self explanatory since it literally means 'propped stone.' In Sino Korean characters it reads Jiseokmyo, which means 'stone grave.'

Northern style dolmen

There are three types of Korean dolmens: The northern, southern and capstone style. The northern style is also known as the table style because of its appearance. It is constructed above the ground and consists of three to four large stone slabs as walls which form a burial chamber. A large and flat capstone would be laid on top of the four supporting walls. The northern type of dolmens are usually found in places north of Han River.

The southern type of dolmens are also known as *Baduk*[1]

1 Baduk: a Korean Chess game played on a checkered board that rests on thick, squat legs.

board style or base type dolmens. The burial chamber is constructed below the ground and the corpse lies in the burial chamber. Several small stones are laid on the ground in the shape of a circle, and a huge capstone is put above the supporting stones. The southern type of dolmens are found south of Han River.

The last type is called the capstone style which is also a below the ground construction. Similar to the southern type of dolmens, the burial chamber is located below the ground as well as the supporting stones. Only the huge capstone is placed above the ground and is visible on the surface. This type of dolmen is distributed mostly throughout the Korean peninsula.

The capstone style dolmen

How were the Dolmens Constructed?

Dolmens were made in a very ingenious way. It is called megalithic culture, which means dolmens are made of huge rocks. The weights of those stones vary from approximately three tons to fifty tons. To make a dolmen, the first thing that people have to do is to find a proper stone and cut it down to the right size. The process of cutting the stones is called quarrying process. The quarrying process involves cutting out the capstone rock; it entails three steps. First, some holes must be bored into the stone after which wooden wedges are driven into each hole. Water is then poured into the holes. By doing so, the wooden wedges become soaked in the holes and expand. Eventually, the big stone is cut into smaller pieces which will be used as the supporting stones and capstone.

Because dolmens are tombs for the chiefs of a tribe, the dead body of the chief is laid in the middle. After laying the body in a room that is surrounded with wooden boards, two long stones are set up to support the whole capstone, which goes on the top. The next step is to pack sand up to the top of the supporting stones, like a mound and on that mound you arrange some logs that enables one to move the heavy capstone. By rolling the capstone on the logs, it can be laid on the top of the supporting stones. This idea of using logs to move the huge capstone is very similar to the process that was used to build the pyramids. After setting the capstone on the top, one has to remove the mound of sand, leaving only the proper dolmen.

Dolmens Scattered all over the Peninsula

There are more than 40,000 dolmens throughout the Korean peninsula with more than 20,000 of them concentrated in the South Jeolla Province. Let's look at the Gochang area first.

1) Gochang Area: Concentration and Mixture

There are more than 2,000 dolmens in Gochang, North Jeolla Province. Starting from Maesan village in Jung-nim-ri, the dolmens are spread from the east to the west, and along the southern foot of the mountain, all within an altitude of 15 to 50 meters. The dolmens in Gochang rank number one in the world in terms of distribution density, with more than 400 in a small area spanning 1.5 kilometers. The dolmens in Gochang are constructed in all three different styles, which makes them even more interesting and historically important.

2) Hwasun Area: A Huge Stone Factory

There are about 300 dolmens in Hwasun, and they are spread along the two valleys of the mountain. The wide flatland around Jiseokgang River, a tributary of the Yeongsangang River, forms the backdrop to this home of the dolmens. They were discovered in 1995, amidst the natural environment of the forest. Thus, the dolmens have been preserved quite well and a nearby quarry where the builders found their stones enabled archaeologists to trace the construction process of dolmens. There are dozens of dolmens in this area that

Southern style dolmen in Gochang area
Baduk board type

weigh more than 100 tons and there are some capstones that exceed 200 tons. Relics unearthed in the dolmens include non patterned earthen vessels, stone arrowheads, stone chisels, stone axes and stone swords.

3) Ganghwa Area: The Largest Table-style Dolmens

There are about 122 dolmens in Ganghwa, concentrated in a 4.0 kilometers radius, which encompass Goryeosan Mountain and the surrounding villages. The most famous of the dolmens in Ganghwa is none other than Korea's biggest table style dolmen, located in Bugeun-ri. It is 2.0 meters tall, with the capstone measuring 7.1 meters in length and 5.6 meters in width. Made of biotic gneiss, a mineral commonly found in Ganghwa, this dolmen is empty inside meaning there is no burial chamber.

What do Dolmens Tell us about Society in the Past?

At first glance, dolmens are just a pile of rocks; it seems as if there isn't much to see. However, the dolmens actually explains a lot about the early civilizations of Korea. For starters, they explain that it was a period when people were no longer nomadic, started to settle down and create

Dolmens in Hwasun Area
Archaeologists traced the construction process of dolmens in Hwasun area where it is considered a huge stone factory.

communities. In order to construct a dolmen lots of manpower was needed as well as time. Depending on the size of the dolmen, a typical dolmen would take a few months to construct. Also, some capstones can weigh a few hundred tons. An experiment conducted in Gochang showed that it took 85 people to carry a capstone that weighed 9.8 tons; it took them four hours to drag it 78 yards! Thus, in order to construct dolmens, an established settlement must be in place.

Dolmens also tell us something about how the settlement works. Dolmens serve for both ritual and burial purposes. Because the construction of dolmens required a lot of manpower and time, only the tribal elite and spiritual leaders were buried in this manner. This shows that hierarchy and class status were established by that time. As for ritual purposes, it shows what kind of lifestyles the people had at that time. For instance, farming was a crucial part of their lives. Ritual farming artifacts show that the people prayed for productivity and a good harvest.

Dolmens are more than just a pile of rocks with burial chambers. These dolmens tells a lot about the society at the time and what the people were like.

Why are the Dolmens Considered a World Heritage?

Gochang, Hwasun and Ganghwa dolmen sites were designated as a World Heritage Site by UNESCO in 2000. As quoted from the UNESCO site, the justification for the inscription is that "The global prehistoric technological and social phenomenon that resulted in the appearance in the 2nd and 3rd millennia BCE of funerary and ritual monuments constructed of large stones (the "Megalithic Culture") is nowhere more vividly illustrated than in the dolmen cemeteries of Gochang, Hwasun and Ganghwa."

Indeed, the Korean peninsula is home to almost 40% of the total number of dolmens in the world. Particularly, Gochang, Hwasun and Ganghwa sites contain the highest density and greatest variety of dolmens. A dolmen is a typical grave during the Bronze Age in Korea, and from them we can infer social, economic and cultural aspects of that time period. Their widespread appearance attests to certain universalities in human nature, particularly with regard to death and burial. They are evidence that even early cultures had the desire and ability to transport and to honor the dead.

In addition, they show how dolmen types changed over time in Northeast Asia. These are of great archaeological value for the information that they provide about the prehistoric people who built them and their social and political systems, beliefs and rituals, arts and ceremonies, etc. They are considered as important relics in tracing the formation and development of dolmens, and they also have unique features incomparable to those in Europe[2], China and Japan.

2
Stonehenge located in England is probably the best known stone monument which shows megalithic culture. Stonehenge was added to the UNESCO's list of World Heritage Site in 1986. The name 'stonehenge' comes from 'stanhengest' which means 'hanging stone' in Anglo-Saxon words. It dates back to 3000 B.C to 1600 B.C. and it is assumed that they had been constructed for 4 times. Then, why was this stones made? No clear reason has revealed yet, we can just guess that it was built for religious ritual.

Reference

Ha, Moon Sig. 2004. A Study of the Dolmens of North Korea - focused on the peculiar structure. *Journal of Korean cultural history*, no. 21, pp. 51–68.

Kim, Gyongtaek. 2004. Emergence of Sociopolitical Differentiation in Korean Prehistory - focusing on the Boseong River Valley in Southwestern Korea. *The review of Korean studies.* v. 7 no. 1, pp. 61–94.

Dolmen Park_Korean Dolmens, http://www.dolmen.or.kr

Gochang County, http://culture.gochang.go.kr/site_english/dolmen/05-01.htm

Gochang, Hwasun and Ganghwa Dolmen Sites - UNESCO World Heritage Centre, http://whc.unesco.org/en/list/977

World Heritage, Hwasun Dolmen Experiential Learning Center, http://www.dolmen.or.kr

Museum

without

Walls

Historic Areas of Gyeongju

Have you ever been to the city of Gyeongju? Maybe you have been there at least once or at least heard of the city. Let me introduce Geyongju to you, "The City of Cultural Assets."

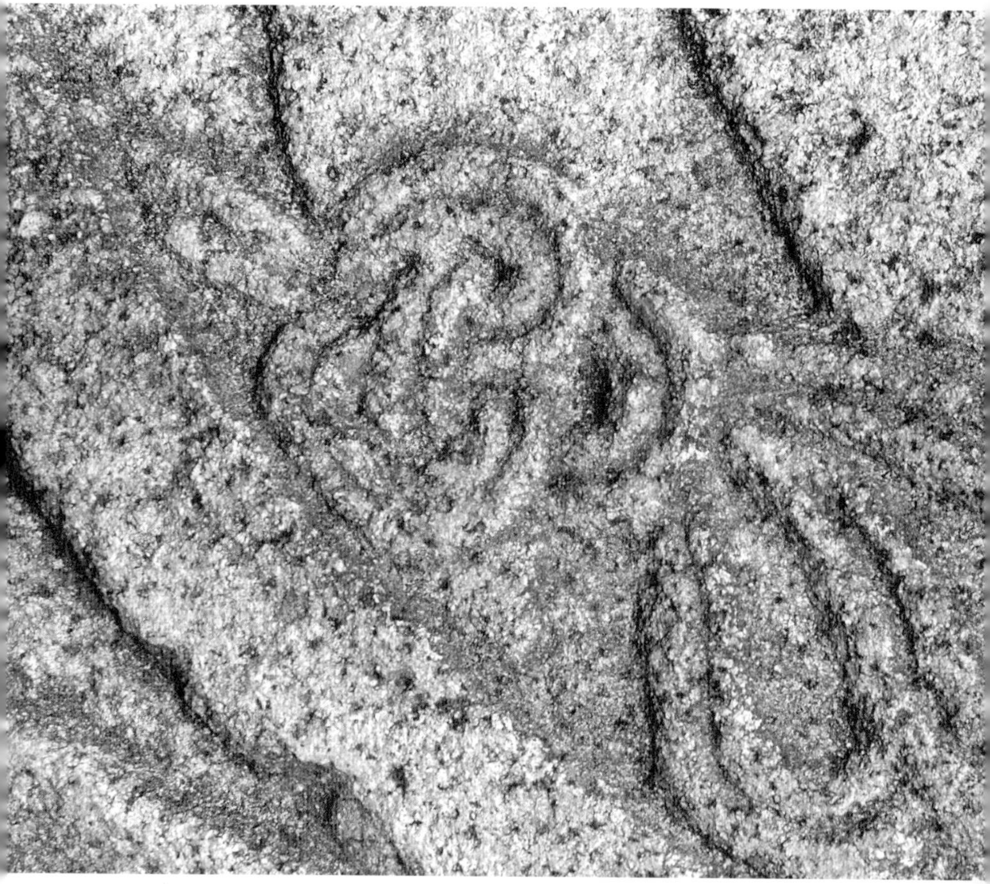

A knot pattern engraved
on a Buddhist statue in
Namsan Mountain

Gyeongju is full of history, art, unique architecture and rich culture that dates back thousands of years. It was the capital of the Silla Kingdom which ruled for more than a thousand years (57 BC-935 AD). Gyeongju was an extremely important capital in the development of Buddhism in Korea. Despite the fact that the religion was adopted in Gyeongju much later than the rest of Korea (527 AD), it certainly gained its strength. There one can find a remarkable concentration of Korean Buddhist art and monuments showing the development of Buddhism and secular architecture throughout the period of Silla.

This is a truly unique aspect of Gyeongju since it continues to hold such ancient heritage of great significance to what is a major religion today. For example in Gyeongju you can find the Seokguram Grotto and Bulguksa Temple, both of which are still highly visited today for their importance to Buddhism. There are also many historic buildings and tombs dating back to the early Korean dynasties such as Anapji Pond, Poseokjeong Pavilion and Seochulji Pond, all of which are part of what was a much bigger palace complex along with many of the royal tombs that are located so near to each other in what is basically the center of the city. It really gives you the feeling of being in that time, and the experience of literally walking through ancient history and a world very different from the one we live in today. So then, let's start our journey to the Gyeongju Historic Areas, one of the largest outdoor museums in the world.

What Historic Sites can be Found in Gyeongju Historic Areas?

Gyeongju Historic Areas contain a remarkable concentration of almost 1,000 years of outstanding Korean culture that is hardly found in any other country in the world. Since Gyeongju bears a large number of national treasures throughout the city, it is almost impossible to pinpoint them all. For this reason, the entire area is registered as a World Cultural Heritage.

There are five major components that make up Gyeongju Historic Areas, namely Namsan Mountain Belt, Wolseong Belt, Tumuli Park Belt, Hwangnyongsa Temple and Sanseong Fortress. The areas contain outstanding examples of Korean Buddhist art in the form of sculptures, pagodas, the relics of temples and palaces that were built between the 7th and 10th centuries, and which have unique forms of artistic expression. The sites and monuments in and around Gyeongju bear outstanding testimony to the cultural achievements of the time. These monuments are of exceptional significance in the development of Buddhist and secular architecture in Korea.

In addition, the tombs of Silla rulers can also be found surrounding the ancient city. Gyeongju is a living history book with well preserved relics of the Silla Kingdom matched in harmony with the natural scenery. By studying the historic sites with the treasures, tombs, palaces, Buddha statues and other relics you are able to understand the history, culture and architecture of the Silla Kingdom.

Namsan Mountain Belt and Buddhism

The Namsan Mountain Belt of the Gyeongju Historic Areas stretches 8 kilometers north and south and 4 kilometers east and west. It links Namsan Mountain with Geumosan Mountain and Gowisan Mountain, and it forms 40 valleys.

The entire Namsan Mountain was designated as Historic Site No. 311. It safeguards some prehistoric remains and a wealth of Silla properties. Najeong, the well that appears in the founding myth of the Silla Kingdom, is in the Namsan Mountain Fortress. Royal tumuli, Poseokjeong Pavilion, with its abalone shaped stone watercourse, and many more make Namsan Mountain a true outdoor museum. The sovereignty and refined culture of Silla have reverberated here down throughout the generations.

The area boasts of an astounding amount of Buddhist relics including 122 temple rims, 53 stone statues, 64 pagodas and 16 stone lanterns excavated so far. There are traces of the early native cultures and nature worship habits as well as the ambition of pious Buddhists to build an earthly Buddha Land on this sacred mountain. Let's examine some of the most representative artifacts.

If you climb around the Samneung Valley you will come across a Buddha image carved on a cliff. This figure is 5.21 meters high and 3.5 meters wide. It is called Sangseonam maedaejabul, and it looks as if Buddha appears from the rock after hearing the prayers of human beings.

Three-Story-Stone Pagoda in the Yongjangsa Valley

Standing on a high knoll on the compound of the Yongjangsa Temple site, this pagoda is visible from every spot in the valley. Although it is only 4 meters tall with missing finials, it looks as if it is soaring up to the heaven. The trimmed natural rock below is designed to make it appear as if the whole mountain is its base. It gives the impression that it connects the sky directly to the earth. Each block is topped by a three layer roof slightly upturned at the end. It is presumed to have been made in the Unified Silla period.

Stone image of a seated Buddha in the Yongjangsa valley

Rock cut Relief of Seven Buddhas on Chilburam Rock

Chilburam literally means "Seven Buddha Rocks." It is composed of two boulders, a larger one with beautiful reliefs of the Buddhist Triad, and before it, a small cubical one with four bodhisattvas. Judging from the fact that a bodhisattva directly faces the main Buddha and has a long torso with shorter legs than the other figures, it can be surmised that they were carved in the 7th or 8th century. The historic site is well preserved and the styles and techniques that were used in this relic are excellent as well. At the top of the mountain there is another stone carved image of Buddha. It is found on the cliff that overlooks a wide panorama of the mountain so the artifact leaves the impression that it is floating in the air. It is amazingly well placed.

Rock-cut Relief of Seven Buddhas on Chilburam Rock

Najeong Well

Bak Hyeokgeose (r. 57 BC-AD 3), the founder of the Silla Kingdom, is said to have been born on this site. One day in 69 BC Seobeol the

chief of Goho Maeul Village saw a white horse kneeling down beside the well. Wondering at this sight he went towards the well, but the horse vanished like smoke. Left behind was only a huge egg. Oddly enough, the egg hatched a baby boy. When he reached the age of thirteen, the chiefs of the six villages voted him as the leader of Seorabeol, the early tribal state that was the cornerstone of the Silla Kingdom. The well in the myth was Najeong. Nobody knows the real story but it is not only interesting but also valuable for comparative mythology.

Wolseong Belt

The Wolseong Belt contains many vestiges of the glory and vicissitudes of the Silla Kingdom: Wolseong, the ruined palace site; Gyerim, the mythical woods in which was born the progenitor of the Gyeongju Kim Clan; Anapji, the pond on the ruined site of Silla's detached palace Imhaejeon; and Cheomseongdae, the oldest astronomical observatory in the east.

Cheomseongdae, the Astronomical Observatory Tower

Cheomseongdae Tower, which means "Star Gazing Tower," was known to be the oldest astronomical observatory in East Asia. It is one of the oldest scientific installations on earth as well as one of the oldest surviving structures in Korea. Cheomseongdae Tower was built during the reign of Queen Seondeok (r. 632-647), Silla's 27th ruler. On a platform of 12 rectangular base stones this astronomical structure is built of 365 granite stones piled up in 30 layers. Many scientists and historians point out that the number of stones, 365, matches the number of days in a calendar year. Some historians also assume that this tower may have been used as a religious symbol or altar rather than an actual astronomical observatory tower because there is not much space for celestial observation.

Tumuli Park Belt

When you visit the city of Gyeongju, you cannot just pass by Tumuli Park Belt because of its huge size. What's more, it is located in the heart of the city which is very unique and cannot be found in any part of the world. Then, why are such huge royal tombs placed in the center of downtown Gyeongju? Historians assume that the size was a display of the royal power.

The Tumuli Park Belt is dotted with clusters of small and large tombs for members of the royal family and the nobility. It is subdivided into the Hwangnam-ri Tumuli, Nodong-ri Tumuli, and Noso-ri Tumuli. Most of the mounds are dome-

A bird's-eye view of Royal Tumuli Park in Gyeongju

shaped. Some are shaped like a half moon or a gourd. In the interior of the mounds consists gravel covered double wooden coffins, stone cists, stone chambers, or burial pits. They have yielded many burial goods showing Silla's cultural quintessence such as gold crowns and diadems, a mural called the "Heavenly Horse," glass cups and troves of earthenware vessels.

Cheonmachong Mausoleum

This mausoleum, 157 meters in circumference and 12.7 meters tall, is presumed to be that of a 5th or 6th century king. Excavation of the tomb revealed 11,500 artifacts, including a mural painted on birch bark of a horse flying to heaven after which this anonymous tomb was named Cheonmachong, the "Tomb of the Heavenly Horse." The tomb was restored as it was found and opened for public viewing through a glass wall.

Hwangnyongsa Belt

This covers the ruined sites of Hwangnyongsa Temple and Bunhwangsa Temple.

Hwangnyongsa was the largest temple ever built in Korea. It was built by order of the 24th king, Jinheung (r. 540-576 AD), in 553; Silla's largest six statues of Buddha were made in 574, the 35th year of the king's reign. The master architect Abijhe of the Baekje King built an 80 meter tall, nine story wooden pagoda in 645, the 14th year of Queen Seondeok, which added sheer magnificence to the stature of the temple. Unfortunately, the statue temple was vandalized during the Mongolian

Sangseonam maedaejabul

invasion in 1238 during the Goryeo Dynasty. Thus, only the ruined site remains.

Sanseong Belt

The Silla Kingdom was the latest to be established among three ancient Kingdoms on the Korean peninsula. Its defense facilities were mostly fortresses along the east coast and at other strategic points aimed to ward off Japanese intruders. Advanced fortification techniques were employed in these structures.

Myeonghwalsan Mountain Fortress

Myeonghwalsan Mountain Fortress was built to the east of Wolseong to safeguard the Silla palace and the eastern outskirts of the capital. The construction date is not clear. Historical records of this fortress state that Japanese warriors were driven away in 405, which at least gives the latest possible date for its construction.

Why is Gyeongju Historic Areas Considered a World Heritage?

The thousand year history of the Silla Kingdom left behind

countless relics. The cultural heritage dating back to the period from the prehistoric age to the Unified Silla era reveals clearly how a culture had risen and declined. Most of all, the relics that were unearthed from the ancient tombs are historic evidences of the heyday of the Silla era.

I'd like to end this brief tour at the Gyeongju National Museum where the famous Great King Seongdeok's Bell is kept. Visitors will be able to hear the echo borne by the winds of a thousand years. "It says: A Holy Bell has been founded, as tall and as proud as a mountain, it sounds like the whispers of a dragon, its echo reaches to the ends of the earth and penetrates the ground beneath. Those who see it will be fascinated, and those who hear it shall be blessed." We cannot imagine the Silla Kingdom without Gyeongju and cannot possibly think of Korean culture without the Silla era.

Reference

Choi Joon-Sik; Sandra Choe (trans.). 2011. *Gyeongju.* Seoul: Hanul.

Jin, K.; Lee, M.; Kim, Y.S. 2011. Archaeoseismological studies on historical heritage sites in the Gyeongju area, SE Korea. *Quaternary international: the journal of the International Union for Quaternary Research.* v. 242, no. 1, pp. 158-170.

Mohan, Pankaj (ed.). 2011. *The Ancient Korean Kingdom of Silla: Political developments and religious ideology.* Seongnam, Korea: The Academy of Korean Studies Press.

The Cultural Property Administration, 1999, *Kyeongju Historic Areas.* World Heritage List Application.

World Heritage List Application, 1999, The Cultural Properties Administration.

Gyeongju City Hall

Gyeongju Historic Area - UNESCO World Heritage Centre, http://whc.unesco.org/en/list/976

Temple of

Buddha Land

and

Buddhist Cave Temple

Bulguksa Temple and Seokguram Grotto

Bulguksa Temple is considered a masterpiece from the golden age of Buddhist art in the Silla Kingdom. The Seokguram Buddha embodies an ideal beauty and is recognized as one of the finest examples of Buddhist sculptures in East Asia. In a word, Bulguksa Temple and Seokguram Grotto are masterpieces that unites science and religion in an unprecedented way.

Let me begin with the Bulguksa Temple.

Why was Bulguksa Temple Built? And What are the Major Features of Bulguksa Temple?

The realization of Buddha Land in the mundane world was a long cherished dream during the Silla Kingdom, so the people decided to build "Bulguksa" which literally means "Temple of Buddha Land." In other words, Bulguksa Temple can be regarded as terrestrial paradise of the land of Buddha.

The grounds of Bulguksa Temple were seen as a utopia of Buddhism itself in the mundane world, and are divided into three areas with wooden buildings on raised terraces, including Birojeon (Vairocana Buddha Hall), Daeungjeon (Hall of Great Enlightment) and Geungnakjeon (Hall of Supreme Bliss). They represent the terrestrial and two celestial abodes, the Pure Land of Buddhism: That is, the terrestrial world of Vairocana Buddha; the paradise of Amitabha; and the World of Endurance of Sakyamuni.

Birojeon, Geungnakjeon, Daeungjeon and the areas on the stone terraces signify the land of Buddha; the lower areas below these terraces are the mundane world. These two worlds are connected by two bridges that are known as Cheongungyo and Baekungyo (Bridge of Blue Clouds / Bridge of White Clouds), and Yeonhwagyo and Chilbogyo (Bridge of Lotus Flowers / Bridge of Seven Treasures).

After first entering the temple, one will see a double sectioned staircase and bridge called Cheongungyo and Baekungyo. There are 33 steps on the stairway which slopes at a 45 degree angle, and each step corresponds to one of the 33 heavens of Buddhism. The lower portion, Cheongungyo (Blue

Cloud Bridge) is 6.3 meters long and has 17 steps. The upper portion, Baekungyo (White Cloud Bridge) is 5.4 meters and has 16 steps. The bridges lead to the Jahamun (Golden Purple Gate), which is the gate to Daeungjeon, the hall of Sakyamuni Buddha. Such a construction is believed to be the only structure that has survived the Silla Kingdom. The symbolic meaning of the bridge like stairwell is the connection between the mundane world below and the Buddha's world above. Some argue that the bridge also symbolizes the life of both a young and old man. The large arch of the bridge testifies that at one time water was flowing underneath the bridge.

To the west, an 18 step stone staircase takes one to Anyangmun (Pure Land Gate) leading to Geungnakjeon, the Hall of the Pure Land. The lower ten-step portion of that staircase is called Yeonhwagyo (Lotus Flower Bridge), while the upper part with eight steps is Chilbogyo (Seven Treasure Bridge). This pair of bridges share the 45 degree incline, arch underneath, and the combination bridge and staircase design of their sister bridges. However, one noticeable difference is that this bridge is smaller. The lower Lotus Flower Bridge has 10 steps while the upper Seven Treasures Bridge contains 8 steps. Both structures are smaller than Cheongungyo Bridge and Baekungyo Bridge, but the design and structure are quite similar.

Yeonhwagyo Bridge is known for its delicate carvings of lotus flowers on each step. It is said that people who have reached enlightenment used these lotus flowers to take their steps towards the Pure Land. However, these have faded with the weight of many pilgrims. Thus today, visitors are restricted from walking on the bridge.

Cheongungyo and Baekungyo Bridge

I am afraid that we have spent too much time outside. There is more interesting information you cannot miss. Let's not waste any more time and get inside the temple.

Upon entering the temple, there stands two pagodas: The one on the left (west side) is Seokgatap, and the other on the right is Dabotap. They are standing in front of Daeungjeon (the main hall) of Bulguksa. While Seokgatap Pagoda represents the spiritual world, Dabotap Pagoda symbolizes the material world. These two pagodas have a great significance in Korean Buddhism.

Now let's take a closer look.

Firstly, Dabotap, also known as the "Many Treasures Pagoda," stands 10.4 meters tall with a highly ornate structure. It is an octagonal pagoda standing on a cruciform base with

Dabotap, meaning "the many Treasures Pagoda"

Seokgatap, Sakyamuni
Pagoda

stone staircases on all four sides and a railing. There used to be four lions standing on the stone staircases of the pagoda but currently only one can be seen. With its excellent craftsmanship, it is hard to believe that the materials used for construction are actually stone. And Dabotap is the only pagoda in Bulguksa Temple that survived throughout time with the structure still intact. Most importantly, Dabotap has shown the artistic essence of the Unified Silla Kingdom using squares, octagons, and circles to build the pagoda. In addition, the length, the width and the thickness are also greatly standardized in every part of the piece.

Next, Seokgatap, or the Sakyamuni Pagoda, stands 8.2 meters tall. Even though the design of this pagoda is more simple compared to Dabotap, it is a good depiction of a traditional Korean style stone pagoda. The design is a three-story pagoda body standing on a two-story platform with simple lines and minimal details. The two-story platform was built strong enough to withstand the whole pressure of the pagoda. The special characteristic is that the tip of the pagoda is circled by several lotus shaped stones symbolizing lotus flowers that fell from the heaven as prophesied in the Lotus Sutra. In 1966, during the restoration of Seokgatap, the Dharani Sutra printed sometime after 704 AD was found inside the pagoda. It is the oldest Buddhist scriptures engraved in wooden blocks.

What is the Uniqueness of Bulguksa Temple?

Artistic, cultural and technological values can be found in Bulguksa Temple. Firstly, the artistic value of Bulguksa Temple is the harmonization of artificial and natural beauty. The location selected for the temple is unique as it expands over both plain and mountain regions. When constructing the foundation of the temple, stone pillars were built into the slope of the mountain. Natural stones were piled up for the lower portion of the pillar and artificial square shaped stones for the upper portion. This created a sense of harmony within the architecture.

Next, we can look at the cultural value of Bulguksa Temple, which houses about ten cultural properties that have been designated as national treasures. Inclusion of so many cultural properties that are considered national treasures within one architectural structure is indeed a rarity.

Lastly, one of the technological values of Bulguksa Temple is the architecture technique used during the construction of the temple. In order to show the harmonization of artificial and natural stones, a traditional Korean construction technique called *Geuraengi*[1] was employed. This technique is commonly used when rendering wooden buildings. The main intention was to preserve the beauty of the natural stones.

In addition, mathematics was applied in all of the architectural designs of the temple. The distance between the buildings, their heights, and their base lengths are all proportionately designed. The basic unit employed to render the dimensions of the architecture of the temple is approximately

1 Geuraengi
The technique that is commonly used when rendering wooden buildings is for preserving the beauty of stones.

half the distance between Dabotap Pagoda and Seokgatap Pagoda. The craftsmen designed and arranged all the temple buildings in a unique manner that complies with this basic unit. This is why visitors can feel the harmonious and symmetrical beauty of the temple from any spot and angle on the temple grounds.

What Makes Seokguram Grotto Special?

Now we turn to another masterpiece in the area, Seokguram Grotto. After visiting Bulguksa Temple many visitors walk up to Seokguram Grotto, just as the pilgrims did. As they say, this can be seen as a spiritual journey into Nirvana in just a short amount of time.

First of all, Seokguram Grotto is entirely man made. The entire building consists of 360 granite stones and no cement was used. The grotto itself is divided into an antechamber and a rotunda, the main hall where the Buddha statue is located. In the antechamber, the eight congregated deities called "Palbujung" guard the hall, and two warriors in martial art poses protect the rotunda.

In the rotunda itself a Buddha statue is located. It is somewhat off centered, some say to let the cave feel more spacious. Surrounding the Buddha are his ten disciples. High up on the walls are ten niches, also called "Gamsil," hut shaped, which formerly contained ten statues that are said to guard the entrance. Nowadays, there are only 8 left. Behind the Buddha, there is a relief of *Gwanseeumbosal*, the eleven faced goddess of mercy. Stone or wooden renditions of the eleven-faced Avalokitesvara are also found in China and Japan, but the Seokguram Avaloitesvara is generally viewed as the most outstanding.

At the center of the granite sanctuary, there is a Buddha statue seated in the main chamber. Seokguram Buddha is highly regarded as a consummate piece of Buddhist art. It is 3.5 meters in height and sits on a 1.3 meters tall lotus pedestal.

The Seokguram Buddha was cut from a single block of granite. The Buddha's left hand rests palm up on his lap while the right hand rest palm down with his fingers extended on his knee. He is sitting in a lotus posture, his right leg crossed over his left. Buddha's eyes are closed and his lips reflect a faint smile. This facial expression brings a peaceful and serene atmosphere to the Seokguram Grotto. On the back of the Buddha sculpture, there is a granite roundel which is engraved with lotus petals. This unique structure, when compared to other Buddha sculptures that are attached to a halo on the back of the structure, unlikely makes the illusion of a halo.

Seokguram Grotto, Korea's largest grotto, is the epitome of Korean Buddhist sculpture. The nearly perfect image of the main Buddha, depicted in a mature, realistic technique, the dauntless images of the Vajrapanis with their fierce glares, the majestic bearing of the *Four Guardian Kings*, the elegantly sculptured *Bodhisattvas* and *Guardian Deities*, and the *Ten Disciples*; each have their own distinct personality and should be masterpieces by any standard.

One of the reasons that makes Seokguram Grotto special is that it is both supremely artistic and religious. It was built scientifically and it is a work of a genius, unparalleled anywhere in the world.

The ceiling of the grotto has an inner radius of 2.47 meters, an outer radius 29.7 meters and has the shape of a half sphere where the height is one meter tall. The ceiling consists of five round layers of granite. At the center of the ceiling there are 125 lotus flower patterned stones making the ceiling weigh over 20 tons. In addition to being heavy, as the granite stone strips are piled more than three layers deep tilting down, there

Seokguram Grotto in 1920s

The Eleven-faced Avalokitesvara: Bodhisattva

It is unique because its crown is adorned with the heads of ten Bodhisattvas and a central Amitabha Buddha.

are two forces at work (the weight of the structure and gravity), that seemingly should cause the structure to collapse. To prevent this, between the connections of the granite strips, 2 meters long key stones were used. By inserting these key stones it creates a momentum of force in the opposite direction, thus achieving an equilibrium of force. In addition, the ceiling was constructed into an exact half sphere shape that helps to form a mechanical balance which makes it very strong and stable.

Seokguram Grotto was built taking into consideration humidity and the air cycle. Korea is a country with a climate of high temperatures and humidity in the summer so controlling the moisture of the grotto is important. If the inside of the grotto gets damp, moss would grow on the surface of the stones which would have made the stones crack. For this, they made a stream flow under the dome. This kept the temperature of the floor more consistent and enabled the moisture to condense into dew on the floor.

Why are the Seokguram Grotto and Bulguksa Temple Considered World Heritages?

Seokguram Grotto and Bulguksa Temple were listed on the UNESCO World Heritage List in 1995 together. Seokguram

Grotto and Bulguksa Temple were constructed during the Unified Silla era. The complex has great historical significance and is a symbol of the Silla Kingdom during an era of rapid development in religion, doctrine, science and arts. The construction and layout of both Seokguram Grotto and Bulguksa Temple included architecture, mathematics, geometry, physics, astronomy, religion and art. For instance, the Geuraengi technique was used to mesh artificial and natural stones together for the fabrication of Bulguksa Temple.

As for Seokguram Grotto, geometry was applied in the placement of the main Buddha statue. Mathematics was used to create symmetry of both complexes in Seokguram Grotto. The usage of white stones for the grotto sculptures was to give the impression of having the Pure Land of Buddha in the present world. The bridges in Bulguksa Temple were constructed based on Buddhist philosophies.

In conclusion, the complex is considered to be a masterpiece of Eastern Buddhist art, which is an outstanding example of the Buddhist architecture of the region.

Reference

Choi, Joon-sik, Kyong-hee Lee (trans.). 2006. *Buddhism: Religion in Korea.* Seoul: Ewha Womans University Press.

Grayson, James H. 1984. "Religious Syncretism in the Shilla Period: The Relationship between Esoteric Buddhism and Korean Primeval Religion," *Asian Folklore Studies*, v. 43, no. 2, pp. 185-198.

Jang, Eunhwa. 2009. *Journey to Korean Temples and Templestay.* Seoul: Her One Media.

Kang, Woobang. 2001. Bulguksa Temple and Seokbulsa Temple. *Korea journal*, v. 41 no. 2, pp. 320-344.

Kim, Lena. 2007. *Buddhist Sculpture of Korea.* Seoul: Hollym International Corporation.

The Korea Foundation. 2010. *Masterpieces of Korean art.* Korea: The Korea Foundation.

Yoo, Myeong-jong. 2009. Temples of Korea : Korean Buddhism, 17 temples of Korea, Buddhism terms. Seoul: Discovery Media, 2009.

The True Record

of the Joseon Dynasty

Annals of the Joseon Dynasty

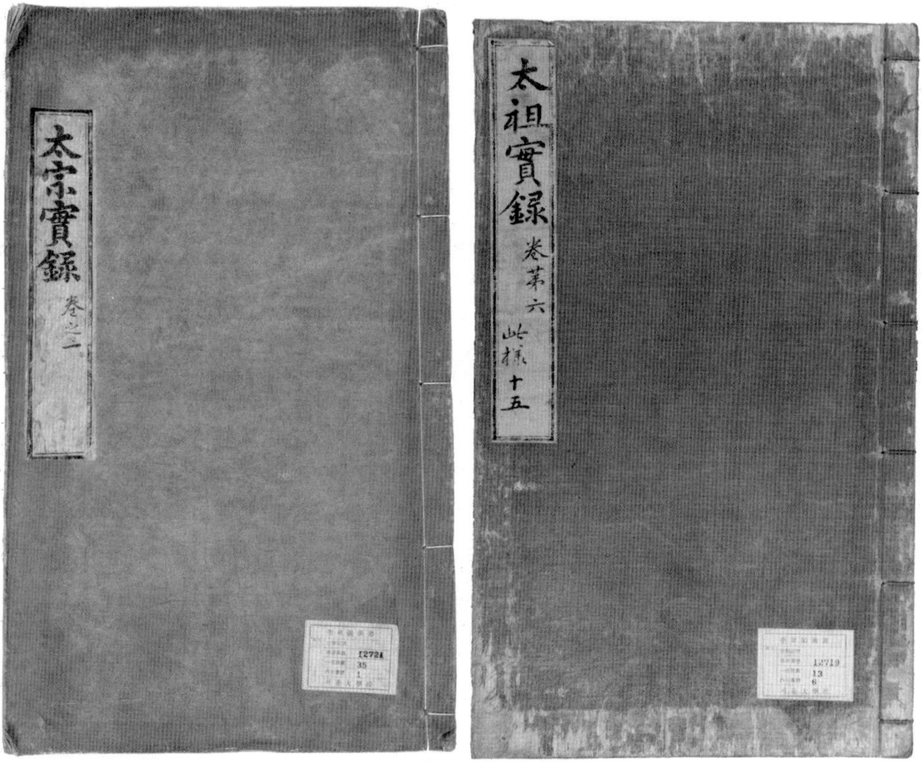

The front pages of Annals of the Joseon Dynasty (King Taejo and King Taejong)

(Source: Kyujanggak Institute for Korean Studies)

Do you keep a daily journal? How long have you continued writing? It is memorable to keep track of your valuable experiences, but you would probably all agree that it is not an easy task to consistently write a diary throughout one's whole life. However, the Annals of the Joseon Dynasty show the detailed annual records of the Joseon Dynasty, which covers 472 years including 25 kings' reigns.

The annals, or Sillok, are comprised of 1,893 volumes and are thought to cover the longest continual period of a single dynasty in the world. With the exception of two annals scompiled during the colonial era, the rest were listed in UNESCO's Memory of the World in 1997.[1] The Annals of the Joseon Dynasty are thought to be an encyclopedia that covers everything about the Joseon Dynasty including its historical facts relvant to politics, diplomacy, law, economies, etc.

Today, annals are used as indispensable materials for the study of Korean history and to aid the study of other East Asian countries like Japan, China and Mongolia.

1
The Annals of the Joseon Dynasty cover the historical and various aspects of the dynasty including politics and diplomacy, military affairs, law, economics, industry, transportation, communications, social systems, customs and manners, arts and crafts and religion. These enormous historical and cultural resources with their unprecedented accuracy serve as an encyclopedic proof of the vastness of the Joseon society.

How were the Annals Written and by Whom?

During the reign of a king, professional historiographers were maintained to keep extensive records on national affairs and the activities of the state. They collected documents and

當以上教起草庸退草之曰不有 卿予爲至此 卿之功與
德予敢忘諸皇天后土在上在旁世世子孫無相害也予所有

負於 卿者有如此盟庸與 殿下進草於恭讓恭讓曰可庸
時無史官書曰上於 侍中扶立之功未報又害之意已萌天
命已去人心已離區區之盟不可賴也

元年(洪武二十五年)秋七月十七日丙申 太祖即位于壽昌宮先是
是月十二日辛卯恭讓將幸 太祖第置酒與之同盟儀仗已
列侍中裴克廉等白王大妃曰今王昏暗君道已失人心已去
不可爲社稷生靈主請廢之遂奉妃教廢恭讓事既定南誾遂
與門下評理鄭熙啓賫教至北泉洞時坐宮宣教恭讓俯伏聽命
曰余本不欲爲君羣臣強余立之余性不敏未諳事機豈無忤
臣下之情乎因泣數行下遂遜于原州百官奉傳國璽置于王
大妃殿庶務就稟裁決壬辰大妃宣教以 太祖監錄國事乙
未裴克廉趙浚與鄭道傳金士衡李濟李和鄭熙啓李之蘭南
誾張思吉鄭摠金仁贊趙仁沃南在趙璞吳蒙乙鄭擢尹虎李
敏道趙狷朴苞趙英珪趙胖趙溫趙琦洪吉旼劉敬鄭龍壽張
湛安景恭金稇柳爰廷李稷李懃吳思忠李舒趙英茂李白由

wrote daily accounts about state affairs as well as diplomatic affairs, the economy, religion, meteorological phenomena, the arts, and even daily lives of the people. These daily accounts became the Sacho (Draft History). Great care was taken to ensure the neutrality of the historiographers, who were also officials with legal guarantees of independence. Nobody was allowed to read the Sacho, not even the king. Also any historiographer who disclosed its contents or changed the content was punished with beheading. These strict regulations allowed a great credibility of the records.

Yet, at least one king, tyrannical Yeonsangun looked into these annals, and this led to the First Purge of the Literati in 1498, for which one recorder and five others were cruelly executed for the contents of the Sacho. This incident caused a tightening of the regulations in order to prevent the king from seeing the annals.

Surprisingly, the recorders were not in a high position in the palace. Nonetheless, they went through strict procedures and only those who embraced a clear historical consciousness were selected. They had to write down everything by following the king at all times. The king was not allowed to discuss national issues with others if there were no recorders by his side. The King's official schedule, national ceremonies, major political events and natural disasters were the affairs that must be reported in the annals; they also cover a diverse range of social phenomena, astronomy, religion, customs, etc.

The actual page of the Annals of Joseon Dynasty (King Taejo)
(Source: The National Institute of Korean History)

How were the Annals Preserved?

When a king died, a temporary office of annals compilation was set up and the annals of his reign were published posthumously and preserved in the historical archives. After having made the compilation, copies were made and deposited in four different mountains in Korea: Jeongjoksan, Taebaeksan, Jeoksangsan and Odaesan. Special buildings were constructed in each location and the copies were sent out.

The Annals of the Joseon Dynasty at first were in manuscript form, and then they were printed with movabletype of bronze and wooden varieties. The annals for the first three reigns, those of Kings Taejo, Jeongjong and Taejong, were in manuscript form in excellent calligraphy. Their system, contents and bindings seem to be of the highest qualities. During the reigns of King Sejong through King Cheoljong, the annals were printed with movable bronze and wooden types. To make the movable type printings in those centuries the best quality of paper, fonts and bindings were used.

Today, there are 2,077 extant volumes that have been handed down. They were collected from the different archives: 1,181 come from Jeongjoksan, 848 from Taebaecksan, 27 from Odaesan and 21 from Sanyeopbon. As the Annals of the Joseon Dynasty were originally written in Chinese characters, ordinary people cannot understand them easily. It took almost 3,000 experts for 25 years (a contemporary Korean edition of the Annals of the Joseon Dynasty was completed in 1993) to translate the Chinese-character annals into Hangeul and to computerize them. Since 2005, anyone can see the entire

2 http://sillok.history.go.kr

text of the Annals of the Joseon Dynasty on the internet.[2] Information can be easily searched according to classification and terminology.

Why was the Annals of the Joseon Dynasty Chosen as a Memory of the World?

The Memory of the World Program was designed by UNESCO in 1992 to ensure the preservation of precious documentary heritage all over the world and to support easier access for researchers as well as interested individuals to increase awareness on the cultural significance of the documents.

As mentioned above, the Annals of the Joseon Dynasty is comprised of 1,893 books covering 472 years (1392-1863) of the history of the Joseon Dynasty. This extensive set of records is considered as a document covering the longest period of a single dynasty in the world. For several convincing reasons, the Annals of the Joseon Dynasty were registered as a Memory of the World.

First, although there are other well known historical documents that cover extended periods of time, the Annals of the Joseon Dynasty are the authentic records of one dynasty, which spans the longest period of time. For instance, the Annals of the Ming Dynasty record the 260 years encom-

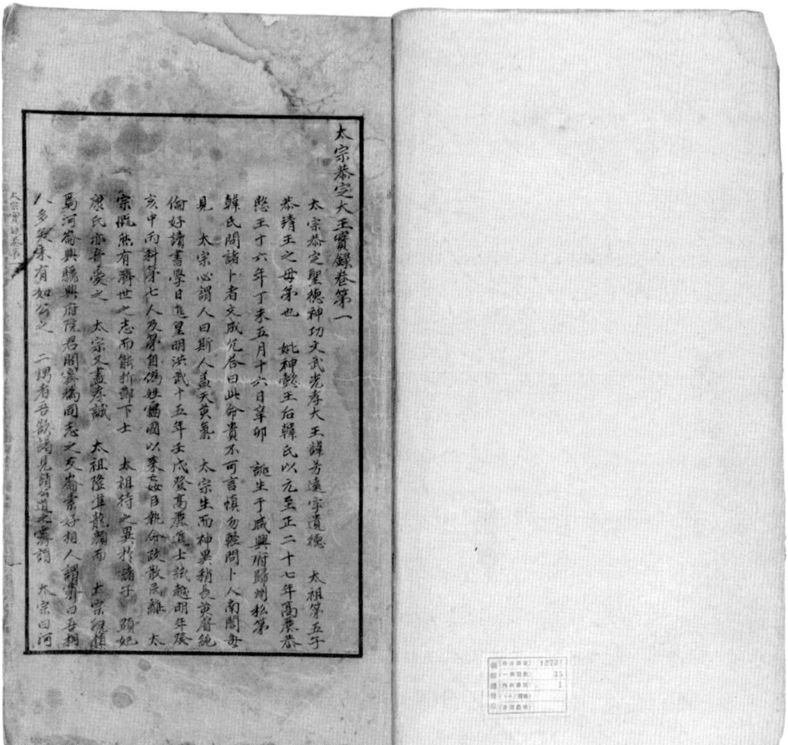
太宗恭定大王實錄卷第一
太宗恭定聖德神功文武光孝大王諱芳遠字遺德　太祖第五子
恭靖王之母弟也　妣神懿王后韓氏以元至正二十七年高麗恭
愍王十六年丁未五月十六日辛卯　誕生于咸興府歸州私第
韓氏問諸卜者文成允答曰此命貴不可言愼勿輕問卜人南誾每
見　太宗必謂人曰斯人蓋天英氣　太宗生而神異稍長英睿絶
倫好讀書學日進皇明洪武十五年壬戌登高麗進士試越明年癸
亥中丙科第七人及第自僞姓竊國以來妾自執命政散民離　太
宗慨然有濟世之志而能折節下士　太祖待之異於諸子　顯妃
康氏亦奇愛之　太宗又盡孝誠　太祖隆準龍顔而　太宗[illegible]
爲河崙與驪興府院君閔霽爲同志之友崙素好相人謂霽曰吾相
人多矣未有如公之二甥者吾欲識見請公道之霽謂　太宗曰河

Sillok of King Taejong
(Source: Kyujanggak Institute for Korean Studies)

passing the reigns of 13 Chinese emperors. Also, there are the Annals of the Great Qing Dynasty, covering 296 years. Yet the Annals of the Joseon Dynasty are unrivaled in the length of time covered.

Secondly, the Annals of the Joseon Dynasty boast the most extensive works containing the greatest variety of historical facts. The contents of the annals are encyclopedic. They include not only the general state affairs but also diplomacy among neighboring northeast Asian countries, politics, the social system, the economy, religion, astronomical phenomena, geography, music, military affairs, transportation and arts, as well as the modus Vivendi of all classes from the royal household to the general populace.

Thirdly, the Annals of the Joseon Dynasty are reliable records based on actual historical facts. The historiographers were professional officials having legally guaranteed independence for their record keepings. Thus, the preservation of the vast collection of annals in almost perfect condition near the end of the Joseon era is unparalleled in the world. This special care under the national system has made it possible today to utilize the cultural and historical heritage of these precious annals.

Finally, the Annals of the Joseon Dynasty are treasured as historic, political and diplomatic materials for research on the relations with Japan, Manchuria, China and the others. The Annals possess great value to the world in casting light on Korea's diplomatic relations with East Asian, American and European countries. Therefore, they must be safeguarded, promoted and opened to the public. By putting more than 20 years of time and energy, the Annals of the Joseon Dynasty in

Korean language have been computerized and become easier to access and read. This is also hardly to be found in any other world history.

Reference

Kyujanggak Institute for Korean Studies

National Memory Heritage Service, http://www.memorykorea.go.kr

The Annals of the Chosun Dyansty, http://sillok.history.go.kr

The National Institute of Korean History

Correct Sounds for
the Instruction
of the People

Hunminjeongeum

訓民正音

國之語音。異乎中國。與文字不相流通。故愚民。有所欲言而終不得伸其情者。多矣。予爲此憫然。新制二十八字。欲使人人易習。便於日用矣。

ㄱ。牙音。如君字初發聲

1
Koreans celebrate the promulgation of Hangeul on October 9th, the day on which Hunminjeongeum was proclaimed.

In 1446, the first Korean alphabet was proclaimed under the name of Hunminjeongeum, which literally means "The Correct Sounds for the Instruction of the People." In fact, this alphabet system was invented in 1443 and it was promulgated after three years of preparation[1]. Bearing the same name, a book was published along with the proclamation to illustrate the principles and explanation in how to use the letters. However, since the 1920s the script has been called Hangeul, meaning "The alphabet of the Han country." Later, the syllable 'Han' began to be interpreted as meaning "great" or "unique."

The principles of forming the 'Hangeul' letters were not known for certain until the original manual of Hunminjeongeum was discovered in Andong city in 1940. Through discovery, the mystery of the orthographic principles underlying the unique writing system of Hangeul was finally solved.

Throughout the world, thousands of spoken languages exist but the number of written languages are not many. Most European countries and African countries such as Swahili use modified forms of the Roman letters to record their words. In this aspect, Hangeul, the indigenous writing system of Korea is truly an epoch making invention.

The origin of most alphabets including Roman and Chinese characters is uncertain or mythological whereas Hangeul is exceptional for its exact origin and background in the history of the writing systems of the world.

The first page of Hunminjeongeum
(Source: Kansong Art Museum)

Portrait of King Sejong, inventor of Hangeul
(Source: King Sejong the Great Memorial Society)

Hunminjeongeum, why was it invented?

King Sejong, the motivating force behind the invention of Hangeul, is considered as one of the greatest rulers in the history of Korea. Highly respected for his benevolent disposition and diligence, King Sejong was also a passionate scholar whose knowledge and natural talent in all fields of study astounded even the most learned experts.

Let's look at the background of Hangeul. Knowing King Sejong, the inventor of Hangeul with his scholars is a prerequisite to better understand the motivating force behind the creation of Hangeul. In the absence of the alphabet system, people during the Joseon era had no choice but to use and borrow Chinese characters which did not correspond to the Korean spoken language. King Sejong felt a great need to create Joseon Dynasty's own alphabet system out of a deep sympathy towards his people who had difficulty conveying their words and thoughts. Thus he was committed to the invention of the writing system so that the common people could easily learn and use it. Such efforts led to the birth of Hangeul, which enabled them to inherit tradition and knowledge and pass it on to the next generation in a written form.

Such a view of King Sejong is literally reflected in the preface of Hunminjeongeum:

"Because the speech of this country is different from that of China, it (the spoken language) does not match the (Chinese) letters. Therefore, even if people want to communicate, many of them cannot state their concerns. Saddened by this, I have (had) 28 letters newly made. It is my wish that every man easily learn these letters and that it be convenient for daily use."

What is the Structure of the Hunminjeongeum?

Let's explore the native alphabet of the Korean language, Hunminjeongeum.

The consonants were formed based on the appearance of 'speech organs' while they make a sound. That is, it was created after observing the changes in the shape of the tongue, lips, teeth and throat while a person pronunciates the sound. ㄱ and ㄴ was modeled after the bent shape of the tongue inside the mouth. The consonant, ㅁ is in the shape of the lips, ㅅ in the shape of teeth and ㅇ in the shape of the throat.

For the vowels, the basic characters ㆍ, ㅡ and ㅣ, were created by modeling the sky, the earth and the people that are said to be the basic elements of the universe.

At the time Hunminjeongeum was created, there were 17 consonants and 11 vowels. However, today, there are 14 consonants and 10 vowels (ㆁ, ㆆ, ㅿ, and ㆍ are no longer used).

In addition to the syllabic structure of Hunminjeongeum, the graphic structure of Hangeul was originally inspired by sinograms, which are not of an alphabetic nature. It arranges every syllable built by letters in a virtual square creating a

ㄱ	ㅋ	ㆁ	ㄷ	ㅌ	ㄴ	ㅂ	ㅍ	ㅁ
ㅈ	ㅊ	ㅅ	ㆆ	ㅎ	ㅇ	ㄹ	ㅿ	

ㆍ	ㅡ	ㅣ	ㅗ	ㅏ	ㅜ	ㅓ	ㅛ	ㅑ	ㅠ	ㅕ

Consonants and vowels of the Hunminjeongeum in 1446

regular alignment. So, the graphic unit is of the syllable and not the phoneme, so one cannot write letters independently. It consists of an alphabet where letters are joined in syllables aligned as sinograms.[2]

2
The contents concerning the next two questions are drawn with the few revision from website information on 'Hangeul' by VANK. See reference VANK (Voluntary Agency Network Korea) http://korea.prkorea.com.

How Can We Classify the Hunminjeongeum Alphabet Compared to Other Alphabets?

Alphabets that are currently used are classified into two: ideograms and phonograms. Ideograms are alphabets where each individual symbol has its own meaning such as Chinese characters. On the other hand, the alphabets in phonograms have specific sounds according to each character or letter. Hangeul and Roman are categorized as phonograms.

Then, let's turn to the characteristics of phonograms. Phonograms are divided into two alphabets: Syllabic alphabets and phonemic alphabets. Japanese Kana is an example of a syllabic alphabets. The characters in Japanese Kana don't make any distinction between the constants and vowels. For instance, one of the Kana characters, 'か (Ka)' is just one syllable which cannot be divided into a constant and a vowel.

On the other hand, phonemic alphabets such as Roman and Hangeul alphabets are considered more developed linguistic systems than Japanese or Chinese in terms of efficiency of using sounds in a language. That is attributed to the fact that phonemic alphabets can make numerous sounds by combining initial sounds, medial vowels and final consonants. For example, a limitless number of words are created only with 24 Korean characters. This is why Hangeul is considered one of the most economical and simple linguistic systems in the world.

What Principles was Hunminjeongeum Based on? What are its Other Linguistic Characteristics?

Hangeul was created based on four principles. First, the principle of the characters is simplicity. The basic formation of consonants and vowels of Hunminjeongeum pursued an extremely concise and minimal form. It is interesting that Hangeul can be structured with the basic figures consisting of a triangle, circle, square, point and a straight line. To this, a stroke could be added for aspirate and fortis, or different characters could be added together, or characters could be written one after another.

Hangeul is sometimes classified as a feature alphabet. The feature alphabets separate one sound from another. For instance, let's take a closer look at some of the Korean alphabet. Both ㅋ and ㄲ are Hangeul alphabets based on ㄱ. We can intuitively know that ㅋ and ㄲ are the alphabets which phonetic features (aspirate, fortis) are added by adding strokes to ㄱ. Therefore, Hangeul is classified into a phonemic alphabet.

Hangeul is a unicameral alphabet, which means a letter is represented only by a single case, contrary to the Latin or Cyrillic alphabets. For example, the sound is simply represented by ㄷ while the Latin alphabet represents it either by the small letter d, or by the capital D. Korean is also an agglutinative and infected language. Its properties (radicals, endings, agglutinations area) are echoed in the writing. Moreover, Korean writing is the only one in Asia to practice spacing between words.

Additionally, the composition of a syllable combines consonants and vowels. The syllable as a letter can be divided into three positions: Initial consonant, vowel and final consonant. In addition, basic forms are shaped in bisymmetric figures on their central axes. This bisymmetric structure offers a sense of balance and stability.

Why was Hunminjeongeum Registered as a UNESCO Memory of the World?

The UNESCO Memory of the World was established in 1992, with the growing awareness to the preservation of, and access to, documentary heritage in different parts of the world. Hunminjeongeum of Korea was registered as the UNESCO Memory of the World in 1997.

Many different groups of people in the world exerted great effort to invent their own writing systems for their language. However, nowhere in the world was there a case of an invention of a new writing system that was not directly affected by or based on an already existing alphabet and then was brought into national use before Hunminjeongeum. Hangeul consists of 24 letters in total, including 14 consonants and 10 vowels. Its form is based on the shape of the speech organs. This was a completely new creation that was not related to any preexisting alphabets. The combination of the letters can make thousands of different sounds.

Furthermore, Hunminjeongeum was the first book ever in the history of the world instructing and explaining a writing system. Linguists around the world praise the well organized fairness of Hunminjeongeum. It is also unique that it contains many historical facts along with the explanation of the alphabets unlike all other books for alphabets. UNESCO designated Hunminjeongeum as a Memory of the World due to its scientific sophistication and the content of it.

Reference

Lee, Chungmin, Greg Simpson and Youngjin Kim. 2009. The handbook of East Asian psycholinguistics. Volume III, *Korean*. Cambridge; New York: Cambridge University Press.

Sohn, Ho-min. 1999. *The Korean Language*. Cambridge: Cambridge University Press.

http://en.wikipedia.org/wiki/Hangul

Kansong Art Museum

King Sejong the Great Memorial Society

The National Institute of Korean Language, http://www.korean.go.kr/eng_hangeul

Bibliography

Kim, Joo-young. 2002. *On the road: in search of Korea's cultural roots.* Seoul: Korea Foundation.

Kim, Sungcherl., Moon Sooyul (trans.) 2007. *World Heritage in Korea.* Seoul: Nulwa.

Lee, Kyong-Hee. 1997. *World heritage in Korea.* Seoul: The Organizing Committee of the Year of Cultural Heritage.

Suh, Jai-Sik. 2011. *World Heritage in Korea.* Hollym International Corporation.

The Center for Information on Korean Culture. 2006. *Exploring Korean History through World Heritage.* Hollym Corp., Publishers.

Yoo, Myeong-jong. 2005. *The discovery of Korea: history, nature, cultural heritages, art, tradition, cities.* Seoul: Discovery Media.

Cultural Heritage Administration, http://english.cha.go.kr/

Official Site of Korean Tourism, http://english.visitkorea.or.kr

UNESCO Memory of the World, http://www.unesco.org/new/en/communication-and-information/flagship-project-activities/memory-of-the-world/homepage/

UNESCO World Heritage, http://whc.unesco.org/

Glossary of Romanization

종묘 Jongmyo

공신당 Gongsindang

사직 Sajik

사직단 Sajikdan

악공청 Akgongcheong

영녕전 Yeongnyeongjeon

잡상 Japsang

전사청 Jeonsacheong

정전 Jeongjeon

제례 Jerye

창엽문 Changyeommun

칠사당 Chilsadang

향대청 Hyangdaecheong

창덕궁 Changdeokgung

경복궁 Gyeongbokgung

금천교 Geumcheongyo

대조전 Daejojeon

돈화문 Donhwamun

반도지 Bandoji

부용정 Buyongjeong

부용지 Buyongji

선정전 Seonjeongjeon

소요암 Soyoam

소요정 Soyojeong

애련정 Aeryeonjeong

애련지 Aeryeonji

옥류천 Ongnyucheon

용화당 Yonghwadang

응봉산 Eungbongsan

인정문 Injeongmun

인정전 Injeongjeon

정의정 Jeonguijeong

정조 Jeongjo

주합루 Juhamnu

취한정 Chwihanjeong

태극정 Taegeukjeong

희정당 Huijeongdang

수원화성 Suwon Hwaseong

거중기 Geojunggi

방화수류정 Banghwasuryujeong

수원부 Suwonbu

실학 Silhak

옹성 Ongseong

장안문 Janganmun

정약용 Jeong YakYong

조심태 Jo SimTae

창룡문 Changnyongmun

채제공 Chae JeGong

팔달문 Paldalmun

팔달산 Paldalsan

화서문 Hwaseomun

화성성역의궤 Hwaseong seongyeok uigwe

해인사 Haeinsa

송광사 Songgwangsa

수기대사 Sugidaesa

장경판전 Janggyeong Panjeon

통도사 Tongdosa

팔만대장경 Palman daejanggyeong

고인돌 Goindol

강화 Ganghwa

고창 Gochang

매산 Maesan

바둑 Baduk

부근리 Bugeun-ri

죽림리 Jungnim-ri

지석강 Jiseokgang

지석묘 Jiseokmyo

화순 Hwasun

경주 역사유적 지구
Gyeongju yeoksayujeok jigu

계림 Gyerim

고호 마을 Goho maeul

나정 Najeong

남산 Namsan

노동리 Nodong-ri

노소리 Noso-ri

두문리공원
Tumuli gongwon

명활산 Myeonghwalsan

박혁거세 Bak Hyeokgeose

분황사 Bunhwangsa

서라벌 Seorabeol

서벌 Seobeol

서출지 Seochulji

석굴암 Seokguram

선덕여왕
Seondeokyeowang

신라 Silla

안압지 Anapji

용장사지 Yongjangsaji

월성 Wolseong

임해전 Imhaejeon

천마총 Cheonmachong

첨성대 Cheomseongdae

칠불암 Chilburam

포석정 Poseokjeong

황남리 Hwangnam-ri

황룡사 Hwangnyongsa

불국사와 석굴암
Bulguksawa seokguram

관세음보살 Gwanseeumbosal

그랭이 Geuraengi

극락전 Geungnakjeon

다보탑 Dabotap

대웅전 Daeungjeon

백운교 Baekungyo

비로전 Birojeon

석가탑 Seokgatap

안양문 Anyangmun

연화교 Yeonhwagyo

자하문 Jahamun

청운교 Cheongungyo

칠보교 Chilbogyo

팔부정 Palbujeong

조선왕조실록
Joseon wangjo sillok

사조 Sacho

산엽본 Sanyeopbon

실록 Sillok

연산군 Yeonsangun

오대산 Odaesan

적상산 Jeoksangsan

정조 Jeongjo

정종 Jeongjong

정족산 Jeongjoksan

철종 Cheoljong

태백산 Taebaeksan

태조 Taejo

태종 Taejong

훈민정음
Hunminjeongeum

한글 Hangeul

김영훈

약력
이화여자대학교 국제대학원 한국학과 교수
이화여자대학교 한국문화연구원 원장
미국 남가주대학교(USC) 인류학 박사
미국 인디애나대학교(Indiana University) 인류학 석사
연세대학교 사회학과 졸업

저서
『문화와 영상: 영상인류학의 이해』, 일조각, 2002
『처음 만나는 문화인류학』, 일조각, 2003(공저)
『韓國人の 作法』, 슈에이샤, 2011

고인돌에서 하늘문까지
한국의 세계문화유산 값 12,000원

2013년 2월 22일 1판 1쇄

저 자 김 영 훈
발 행 인 임 삼 규
발 행 처 **지 문 당**
주 소 10881 경기도 파주시 광인사길 85(본사)
03134 서울시 종로구 돈화문로 82(서울사무소)
등 록 1997. 12. 30. 제406-2003-000038호
영 업 부 (02)743-3192~3 팩스(02)742-4657
전자우편 sale@jimoon.co.kr
편 집 부 (02)743-3096~7 팩스(02)743-0227
전자우편 edit@jimoon.co.kr
홈페이지 www.jimoon.co.kr

ISBN 978-89-6297-146-0